P9-ECN-689

LADIES NIGHT
AT THE
DREAMLAND

John Griswold, *series editor*

ALSO BY SONJA LIVINGSTON

Ghostbread

Queen of the Fall

LADIES NIGHT
AT THE
DREAMLAND

SONJA LIVINGSTON

THE UNIVERSITY OF
GEORGIA PRESS
ATHENS

Published by the University of Georgia Press
Athens, Georgia 30602
www.ugapress.org
© 2016 by Sonja Livingston
All rights reserved
Designed by Kaelin Chappell Broaddus
Set in by 10.7/13.5 Fournier MT Std MT Regular
Printed and bound by Thomson-Shore, Inc.
The paper in this book meets the guidelines for
permanence and durability of the Committee on
Production Guidelines for Book Longevity of the
Council on Library Resources.

Most University of Georgia Press titles are
available from popular e-book vendors.

Printed in the United States of America
16 17 18 19 20 C 5 4 3 2 1

Library of Congress Control Number: 2015957597

ISBN: 978-0-8203-4913-8 (hardcover : alk. paper)
ISBN: 978-0-8203-4914-5 (e-book)

FOR JIM

Imagination, then, must be the flip side of memory,

not so much a calling up as a calling forth.

— JUDITH KITCHEN

CONTENTS

The Dreamland • 1

Sly Foxes • 7

We Ghosts • 19

Some Names and What They Mean • 27

A Thousand Mary Doyles • 39

Mad Love: The Ballad of Fred and Allie • 43

Dare • 57

The Goddess of Ogdensburg:
A Rise and Fall in Seventeen Poses • 63

Big • 79

Manuela, with a Hip • 87

On Seeing Weather-Beaten Trees:
A Study in Two Photographs • 99

Heroines of the Ancient World • 103

Twyla · 115

The Opposite of Fear · 119

Human Curiosity: A Circular Concordance · 131

The Second Morning · 139

Rosalie, from the Philippines · 147

Blue Kentucky Girl · 153

The Other Magpie · 163

Freeze-Frame · 175

A Girl Called Memory: A Triptych · 183

Return to the Dreamland · 187

Acknowledgments · 195

Sources · 197

AUTHOR'S NOTE

This is a work of literary nonfiction. While the essays don't stray beyond historical parameters, imagination and supposition are used to explore subjects' lives within that context. In the personal components of the work, some identifying information has been changed to protect the privacy of others.

LADIES NIGHT
AT THE
DREAMLAND

THE DREAMLAND

In my imagination, it still stands.

Out on Ontario's southern shore, a wood-floored pavilion built over a ravine, near the roller coaster, boardwalk, and promenade of games. The dance hall burned to the ground in 1923, but, in my mind's eye, the Dreamland remains a place of laughter, filled with women with newly bobbed hair who rise and spin with partners before the orchestra.

A breeze comes up from the shore, fluttering dresses and ties, and what a fine place it is, situated on the headlands of the smallest Great Lake near the beach where bootleggers unload crates of whiskey brought over from Canada, a place for people from the nearby city to escape the summer heat. Connected by trolley to the carousel and grand hotel down the shore, the dance hall is part of the "Coney Island of the West," but then, the actual Coney Island has a Dreamland too—inhabited by a one-armed lion-tamer, a slew of acrobats, and a replica of Venice, complete with gondolas and a Bridge of Sighs.

The downstate Dreamland was also lost to flames, so that, in both cases, the Dreamland belongs to the past, except as it exists in these pages. And even here it's a passing fancy—its wood floor and bandstand—constructed of memory and imagination to hold the girls and women in this collection.

I conjure them—daredevil and poet, singer, slave and social reformer, misfits and models, and girls snatched away in broad daylight—making use of the old stage, shining a light on each as they saunter by, some in silks and chiffons, others in work clothes and old winter coats. They rub their eyes after so much sleep, the little ones looking with longing toward the carousel. Most lived extraordinary lives—sometimes as victims but also as rule-breakers, their differences thrusting them into view—but even then, views of them were fleeting or faulty so that their relative obscurity is the real story. Some have names you'll recognize, while most are shadowy figures lost to time, women and girls slipping through the world largely unseen.

Here, they take center stage, in essays as diverse as the women they highlight. Some pieces are largely personal, others are poetic renderings of the historical, and many are mash-ups of both. The subjects range from the time of the English colonists to present-day America, with several essays functioning as hybrids not situated in any one era. Many make use of speculation, as in "Mad Love," which tells the story of a Memphis society girl who murdered her female lover in 1892. Some follow a traditional narrative, while others experiment with form; a piece about Krao Farini—a child exhibited as a curiosity in the late nineteenth century—takes the shape of a brief concordance, and an essay inspired by the artists' model Audrey Munson arranges itself into a series of seventeen poses. The essays are organized as connective threads but need not be read in order. A handful of subjects intersected directly with my life, while most showed themselves in slivers and bits. But whether they were channeled through half-remembered history lessons, the pages of a newspaper, or the scratch of an old record, each of these women and girls showed herself when I called—coming so close that, at times, I could nearly feel her beside me as I wrote.

Which brings us back to the Dreamland, where a woman in a silk dress steps up from the dance floor, an orchid pinned to her dark curls, her stride so graceful she nearly floats to the stage, which throws its light into a halo around her. She stands before the orchestra, and the men in their white jackets do their best to remember their instruments once she opens her mouth. It's an old song, all horn and swing, a familiar tune, the rhythms mixing with something clean and sweet—perfume climbing from wrists and knees, sprigs of mint leaves stashed under the makeshift bar. The sound unfolds into the night, dipping and rolling, the pull of trombone and flight of strings, the women in their shimmer dresses, the moon guiding bootleggers into the bay.

The dancers turn as the singer's voice cascades over the clink of glasses, eyes closing as she sings the refrain—something about stardust and twilight.

A place of possibility, the Dreamland, where nothing is truly lost.

A place to stretch my legs and consider those who've gone before me, lives I've pondered and most wanted to know. A place to call out names and listen for voices I might recognize. A place to sit back and watch in wonder as they begin to flicker past, one at a time, the first of them heading now into the spotlight.

The Erie Canal boom in the early nineteenth century helped turn central and western New York State into a hotbed of social reform, sparking movements for women's rights and abolition, utopian experiments, and widespread religious revivals. Figures such as Susan B. Anthony, Elizabeth Cady Stanton, and Frederick Douglass populated the region, as well as religious pioneers such as Joseph Smith, founder of the Latter Day Saints, and William Miller, the founder of the Millerites, who predicted that the second coming of Christ would take place October 22, 1844—a date later known as "The Great Disappointment." Into this fervor in 1848 came two girls from Hydesville.

SLY FOXES

It must have been Maggie who started the thing. The older of the two, it was natural that she would take the lead. But there was something in the younger girl's face—a bit of fire behind Kate's eyes, a certain boldness to her features—that leaves room for question. At twelve, Kate still wore her dark hair in braids, while Maggie would have begun pulling hers into a bun and binding the new curves of her body into a corset. But whether they were more rightly called children or young ladies, they were sisters, sharing the same rooms, tangled together in bed, repeating the rumors they'd heard: there had been a murder years before in the very same rooms in which they now lived.

1848. Hydesville, New York. There was no lack of gloom in the era: typhoid and consumption, losses of women and babies in childbirth, stories of the thousand workers who'd died from malaria in the nearby Montezuma Swamps while extending the Erie Canal a generation earlier. The Fox sisters grew up listening to such accounts. Add to that talk of murder in the house that the Fox family now occupied, and there was no shortage of shadows slipping along walls, no dearth of branches tapping at windows. The girls pushed together against the dark, noticing the power of such talk—the way electricity shot through the body, gathering the skin into shivers, the way normally perfunctory adults went wide-eyed when such tales were exchanged but exchanging them anyway, partaking in a sort of terrible glee.

This is how they come to me: Kate squirming before a looking glass as Maggie urges her to be still and brushes out her hair, discussing the most recent account, wondering out loud about the murder.

"Which room, do you think?" Maggie asks, and Kate raises her eyebrows in mock wonder to indicate their own. Both girls push the story a bit, and the space between imagination and desire blurs until the room goes cold and one says to the other, "Did you hear that?" and the girls scramble into bed, chattering and breathless.

"A ghost," they whisper. "A bona fide spirit of our very own!"

"Noises, like knocking," they later report to their parents, who, because they are doting or suggestible or perhaps even enterprising, claim to hear the sounds themselves. The entire Fox household begins to speak of the thud of objects in the night, the patter of unexplained feet, the feel of cool hands pressing on their faces. The family repeats their stories to friends and neighbors, and word spreads of the Fox family's ghost, the one that Maggie and Kate first heard. And while it was the girls who first laid claim to the spirit, the sisters simply gave form to what was already stirring in the air.

I was nearly the same age as the younger Fox sister the year I met Michelle Labella. 1979. Thirty miles west of Hydesville, in Rochester, New York—the urban center of a region of lazy foothills bottoming into wetlands, a mild landscape south of Lake Ontario, leafy green and buzzing in summer, frozen over in winter.

I'd always been a spooky sort, the first to volunteer for Ouija board games or to join the séances a cousin loved to organize, listening hard to stories of those who refused to stay dead: *John F. Kennedy*, *Bloody Mary*, and *the White Lady*. I left behind such talk when I met Michelle, a girl whose primary interests were lipstick, disco music, and the ever-present possibility of romance. Michelle courted drama and was a devotee of intrigue, but she did not go in for ghosts—though perhaps more than anyone, Michelle Labella understood the divide between the seen and the unseen world.

I met her at church, the tallest girl to ever walk through the arched wooden doorway of Corpus Christi—a giantess wearing a red halter top, leaning her body like so much new fruit against the altar rail. Earrings dangled to her shoulders, her painted eyelids were so shuttered with lashes they resembled a cow's, and like a cow, the girl wore an indolent expression on her face, chewing pink bubble gum and lowering her lids from time to time, as if bored by the golden-guitared folk Mass, as if unaware her body was a flare.

She might as well have been the ghost of John F. Kennedy for how shocking she appeared against the altar rail. I looked around for confirmation of the apparition but found no other eye. There was no wrong way to be at Thursday night Mass—our free-thinking priest invited parishioners to gather around the altar. Teens straddled the spaces along the collapsing marble rail, and everyone liked how liberal it felt to gather in faded blue jeans and cotton sundresses in spaces normally reserved for the sacred. But the girl in the red shirt was something else. We kept on singing folk songs despite the shift in the air. Women forced themselves into wide smiles or blindness depending on their levels of charity, while men tried with less success to master the same tactics. I could not look away from the girl snapping her gum, seeing but mostly feeling the way the world shrank in her presence, the way other girls became suddenly microscopic, bland as cooked peas in the face of a bottled cherry.

Mr. Splitfoot is what the Fox sisters called their ghost, styling their spirit as no less than Lucifer himself. Kate was the first to address him directly.

"Repeat the sound of my hand snapping," she demanded, and lo and behold, the devil himself was dutiful as a child and did as he was instructed. The sisters devised a code, a certain number of knocks for *yes* or *no*, eventually an entire alphabet with which to communicate.

Will the night be a cold one? they might have asked.

Oh tell us, Mr. Splitfoot, can we expect a heap of snow?

But I suppose their questions would have been less trifling. Teenagers may not have existed as a concept for Victorians, but the terrain between child and woman was no less dramatic for lack of category, and according to the girls' claims, a man, though disembodied, lurked about their room at night. Their questions would have been delivered with flourish, with the topics weightier than lake-effect snow.

On the matter of a murder in our humble abode, what say you, Mr. Splitfoot?

And perhaps the questions are not so important, for it was the answers that Hydesville began to speak of. Responses delivered to the girls in a series of knocks.

The little hamlet bent its ear toward the Fox home. All of Wayne County began to speak of it. "The voice of a dead man," people whispered, "and chatting to our very own Maggie and the little one Kate!"

By the time word spread through Hydesville, the Fox sisters had stopped addressing their spirit as Splitfoot and developed a fuller account of his story: He was named Charles. He'd been a peddler. His body was buried in their cellar.

So seriously were the girls' accounts taken that men carried shovels into the Fox home to dig into the cellar, searching for the peddler's remains. Only a few animal bones were found in the dirt, but such a small detail could not derail the train already set in motion.

When Michelle Labella extended an offer of friendship, I acted out my gratitude by following blindly into a land of mascara wands, teased hair, and knock-off designer jeans. More than a century after the Fox sisters had demanded a response from their spirit, we channeled a bit of their moxie and made ourselves into foxes. Michelle and her two older sisters loved music—disco, funk, and soul—and started a dance group called the Sly Foxes with their friends, all teenagers, except me. No one ever considered the need for a dance group or where we might perform. The focus was on the choosing of names, the design and ordering of baby-blue monogrammed T-shirts—"The Sly Foxes" plastered in Art Deco lettering across our backs. The shirts and deciding which songs to dance to during practice sessions in the church hall after Mass were the entire point.

The older girls laid out the moves, choreographing steps to Sister Sledge and Curtis Blow, directing our bodies to the beat of "Hot Stuff."

Seven or eight girls arranged into three rows. Michelle insisted on the front, dead center, which was the right place for her, with her Sly Foxes shirt stretched over her bountiful chest, the exaggerated movements, the drama of heavily shadowed eyes. I danced in the back, the youngest and shortest, all slippery hair and soft belly, the body of an expectant child.

While I hated being the baby, I was, at least in part, more comfortable in the back row—the impulse to hide loomed larger in me than the desire for a foxier position. Even in moments of prettiness—others complimenting my hair or eyes so that I occasionally slipped into the wondrous terrain of beauty—even then, I understood that beauty came in different flavors, and no matter how much I might wish otherwise, I'd never be a cherry.

Seen and not heard. Taken from the Old English, the saying was originally directed toward young ladies: *A maiden should be seen but not heard.* Whether meant to include children from the get-go or extended over time to include them, in March 1848, Kate and Maggie Fox were both children and maidens, and the adage would have applied twice.

Seen and not heard.

How to account then for the grown men and women leaning in to hear? How to explain Kate and Maggie standing in front of a crowd, all of Hydesville hanging on their every word?

The Fox sisters gave their first public demonstration at Corinthian Hall in Rochester in late 1849. In their spirit session, tables moved of their own accord, and great rumbles were heard throughout the hall as Maggie and Kate called out to spirits, asked questions, and translated answers from the great beyond. The audience was riveted—a general buzz rose from the assembly, the bench and floor creaked as people leaned in, the girls commanding every uptake of breath.

Twenty years older than Kate and Maggie, their sister, Leah, was well-connected in the city and pivotal in her sisters' fame, spreading word of their gift to her Rochester friends and presenting the girls in the homes of acquaintances, including progressive Unitarians and Quakers. Not everyone believed, of course, and commissions were later appointed to investigate fraud, but no one was able to detect trickery in what came to be called the "Rochester rappings."

As word of the rappings spread, the sessions were repeated, again and again, until those wanting seats outnumbered the capacity of local exhibition halls, and the girls headed east to New York City.

The first time I took center stage was before I met Michelle Labella. Show Night at sleep-away camp. A bunch of inner-city kids bused out to open fields, sleeping in cabins and running along a soft slip of sand near Lake Ontario. We learned to boondoggle and sing campfire songs. Show Night was held on the last night of camp, the highpoint of the week. Kids practiced juggling and magic tricks and asked each other what acts they might perform. For a variety of reasons, the desire to hula was large in me, and I recruited the toughest girls at camp as backup dancers.

"Why do you hang out with those girls?" My sister Stephanie noticed the way they talked back and picked fights, and shook her head. To me, the appeal was clear. I was quiet, yes, but not without ambivalence. I wanted their fire and sass, and my wanting was not in vain because some of it rubbed off as the three of us practiced hula dancing on the pebbled shore of Lake Ontario. On the appointed night, we strutted toward the stage—assured by how smooth we'd been as we practiced behind the curtain, shaking with rhythm, our hands becoming birds, the tumble of three pairs of straight hips.

The lights in the craft barn blazed as our act was introduced and we reached center stage, the faces of campers and counselors were expectant, and just like that, legs that had so recently learned to strut turned to stone. The emcee said my name again, our names, for we were a trio, me out front, the bad girls providing a backbone. Except there was no backbone. The music started up: *My little grass shack in Kealakekua, Hawaii*—the lonely sound of the record turning under a needle, the song sounding thin without our dance to keep it company, the weight of so many eyes and the three of us frozen onstage, all badness evaporated under the glare of light.

That I preferred to hide from view was nothing new. I blushed when called upon in class. My knees knocked when I stood to read from the Bible on my First Communion day. How much easier to be a girl who fades into the background, like the daisy I played in the first-grade play, with a circle of yellow petals cut from construction paper stapled and set around my face. I had not minded, not with all the other flowers for company.

Seen and not heard.

A good and quiet girl. A wallflower. But even as I took root against the edges, I watched and wanted something of the swingy-hipped cherry bombs who refused to fade into the background, Michelle, her sisters, and all the other foxes.

The Fox sisters could not have imagined something so large when whispering about Mr. Splitfoot in 1848, but what a delicious hook their spirit sessions became, how far they went. Two girls headed off to the city, making and keeping their own money, not marrying until they wanted to, never once accepting the back row.

Progressives were some of the earliest converts to the public séances and the beginnings of the religious movement that would become known as Spiritualism. Staunch supporters of abolition and women's rights, they were tired of waiting for the established churches to take up their causes with meaningful vigor and were primed for something new. And just like that, the Fox sisters came before them, all gleaming eyes and shining hair, sitting in front of crowds, speaking to those no one else could see, saying that anything was possible, that nothing was gone forever—can there be anything so captivating in all the world?

One of my last adventures with Michelle was a trip to Rochester General Hospital for a pregnancy test. *Why all the way to a hospital for a test? Had there been a boy? Had she missed her period?* These are questions neither of us asked, as Michelle, impatient for life to take off, orchestrated the entire affair. I was cast in the role of mother. A foot shorter than Michelle and flat-chested, my long hair flapped into a face made more babyish for lack of mascara and lipstick.

"What?" I said, somewhere between flattered at the idea that I could pull off the role of adult and shocked at her delusion of the same. She begged, tremendous tears forming in her blue eyes and rolling onto the carpet as we faced each other, lying on our stomachs, the sound of Elton John singing "Little Jeannie" coming from the radio in the kitchen.

"But Michelle," I said, "no one will believe I'm your mother."

"You'll wear heels." She winced, as if my words had hurt her. Her breath was ragged, and black trails of mascara ran the length of her cheeks. "And makeup."

We took a city bus to Portland Avenue, and it's possible she talked her oldest sister into coming along—the most important details are foggy, and such facts hardly mattered. Michelle's scare was like the dance group, the Sly Foxes. It was all about dressing up and pushing ourselves onto a stage—any stage—even one of our own making.

On the morning of the pregnancy test, Michelle ripped through her closet and settled on a beige shirtdress that hung to my ankles. She pulled my hair into a bun and used a curling iron to make ringlets of tendrils that slipped out while snapping her gum and lamenting the fact that my ears were not pierced. As for me, I let her pay my fare and followed her onto the city bus. During our ride, I looked out the window and worried whether, at twelve years old, I might possibly manage to convince anyone I was the voluptuous teenager's mother.

The girls had their detractors: those who claimed that the Fox sisters and their sessions were frauds. Harry Houdini devoted much energy to trying to debunk their claims, while others let themselves believe. By the end of the nineteenth century, Spiritualism had attracted nearly eight million followers, including such prominent figures as Horace Greeley, Sojourner Truth, and Arthur Conan Doyle. Mary Todd Lincoln even hosted a séance in the White House, attended by the president himself. Grief-stricken over the loss of her sons, the first lady was especially receptive to voices from the unseen world. As was the nation perhaps, with so many brothers and sons lost in the War between the States. People were primed to gather in parlors, close their eyes, and wait for the sound of loved ones to speak to them, if only just one more time.

I don't remember much of the hospital adventure with Michelle, except that I entertained myself by following the line of blue tape down corridors and staring into the gleam of metal elevators while she was off in other rooms. There was no pregnancy, of course. There was probably not even intercourse.

"Thank God," she would have said while slipping into the molded plastic seat of the Portland Avenue bus and refreshing her lipstick. "That was a close call."

It's the bus ride to the hospital that's stayed with me. That moment of pushing forward, the possibility of getting caught and becoming the focus of so many eyes, the cool authority of doctors and nurses, their white coats and clicky pens, the way I'd tried in my own quiet way to stop our going but knew there was no turning back. Me, in an ill-fitting dress and shoes I could barely manage, praying against the very same thing Michelle spent her energy in pursuit of, the thing I tried my best to cultivate, but which remained a mystery. How I admired the way she grabbed hold of the world with her red satin blouse and wild bag of stories. Even as my gut knotted and I understood that such things would never quite fit—how much I wanted them just the same.

As in the best of stories, it came down to a girl with an apple. Two girls, in this case.

An apple on a string, one of the Fox sisters later confessed, claiming to have stashed the fruit under her skirts. They learned to drop the apple at just the right moment, and to crack the knuckles of their toes. Later, she recanted her confession, insisting that the voices they had channeled were real. But by the time the Fox sisters made such revelations and redactions, the years had rolled forward and the facts no longer mattered.

It began with them, but the words they spoke acquired a force of their own as soon as they'd left the girls' mouths, sweeping the nation at a time when ghost stories mingled with talk of equal rights and new ideas about how to make sense of a rapidly changing world. The Fox sisters' words had caught fire, but the girls were merely the tinder from which the great blaze came.

In the end, it does not matter so much whether it was an apple dropped from inside a skirt, the crack of knuckles, or the girls communicating with an honest-to-God ghost. It does not matter whether Michelle took an actual pregnancy test or simply roamed the corridors in another wing of the hospital, following her own path of taped lines. In retrospect, it's easy to see that Michelle's display of her body against the altar rail was a cry for much-needed attention—she was a girl whose mother had been as permissive as her father had been harsh, so that when he left, his daughters were left to pucker and spin in the manner of their choosing. As for the Fox sisters, their acts might have been based on trickery, desperation for a voice, or something else altogether.

What matters most is the way each of those girls created and stood on their respective stages at a time when the world would have preferred they remain silent.

Seen and not heard.

They were having none of it and took their places, mouths swollen with secrets as they fluttered their lashes. Brazen young things.

It was something new at least: the people at Corinthian Hall becoming used to the sight of girls outside parlors and kitchens. Parishioners at a folk Mass watching as a girl in a red satin blouse settles against the altar, a real-life woman making herself at home at the center of the church, the quieter girls leaning in and taking note as the world, on its slow magnetic pole, readies itself for the sound of new voices.

Our bones ache only while the flesh is on them.

— DJUNA BARNES

WE GHOSTS

Can't help but pity the living, the way they gather moonfaced over spirit boards, words tumbling from open mouths as they follow the glide of planchette, praying for answers to their warbled demands:

Come now, lil' Chloe.

Show yourself, Miss Jenny.

Give us one last kiss, sweet Lydia.

As if ghosts are cats crouched just under the porch steps. As if we require the living like lantern light to guide us back home. And when we show, dip even a toe into the realm of the living, the way they carry on, shouting, *Sweet Jesus*, and *Lordamighty*, falling to the floor in giddy fits over the scent of jasmine come now into the room. What a show, the séance crowd, sighing till their lungs deflate, hoping so hard their bodies topple in heartache. All while we stretch our legs and recline, counting on ringed fingers as the years slip past, humming the tune to "Mr. Sandman" while wondering what we have a taste for tonight.

We ghosts were once girls who took a spin in a reality machine and looked back on our lives, turning our lips at the shape of our old skins—is there anything so eye-opening as death? A ghost is a girl grown round, a pot of *puttanesca*, all tomato, fish parts, and spice. We no longer consult with our daddies before making a move on the world. A ghost does not worry whether she piles too much on her plate, nor does she hesitate to run her hand over the sleeping plank of a man, saying out loud, *now I'm gon' get me some.*

We slop soup and slap loud against lovers, then disappear once we've had our fill, clomping on heels strapped to feet we don't need as we parade across hardwood and cool marble tile. A ghost is a woman so tired of holding her tongue she becomes nothing but tongue, slick arc of pink, licking the world that once licked her flat.

Here comes little Chloe from West Feliciana Parish: a child walking among live oaks, Spanish moss moving like white girls' hair in the breeze that sometimes comes up from the river. Just a girl when Master scooped her up from the fields, saying, *Now you'll be in the big house*, and in the big house she was, all papered walls and starched sheets. Chloe was a near-princess twirling through rooms with high ceilings topped by carved cream molding so that it seemed she was living inside a wedding cake. She learned to smile and twist her behind at just the right time, and all was fine, until something shifted, Master sniffing out someone new or Chloe letting that little bit of love get to her, acting bigger than she should, sneaking into the lady's closet and sweeping soft fabric against her cheek. Something changed, alright, but even Chloe knew that a person can't ever go back to field and shack, so she took to creeping at keyholes, stealing bits of Master's business, until she was caught. The golden shell of her ear was taken as punishment.

Psshaw, said Chloe. *Who needs both ears?* She wound a green turban around the rest of her pretty head and was given work in the kitchen—not the field at least but still a few steps removed from the house. She hatched a plan. She'd bake a cake and lace it with oleander leaves—a poison, but Chloe knew the cure, and saving some lives—well, that would make Master trust her again, his good girl Chloe. And yes, she was two parts desperation to one part reckless, and the white babies ate that cake and died, Miss Sara and her children. They hanged Chloe. The scent of oleander was still on her skin when they cut her down. They tossed her body into the Mississippi, where it should have floated like a broken branch to New Orleans and out into the Gulf.

But Chloe was not the sort to stay in a river. She rose up, wrung the muddy water from her curls, and slipped back to the big house just like years before when she was new, with Master pressing into her flesh, her serving up fresh fruit in bed and waiting on his wife. But, of course, that's all old news, and Chloe no longer does anyone's bidding. She's down there now, in West Feliciana Parish, queen of the entire house, no one telling her which thresholds she can or cannot pass.

Neither can anyone tell Miss Jenny of Harpers Ferry what to do. Miss Jenny, like other poor souls, took shelter in a storage shack along the railroad tracks. In her day, Miss Jenny of the railroad shack was the best sort of woman, giving away what she had even when it meant she wouldn't eat. How the world likes to make reports of such women, because if Jenny can hole up in a shack without penny or proper coat and share her last bite—see here, sister, imagine what you could do. But oh no, now it's winter. The leaves have fallen, snow settled into the crooks of mountains, the Potomac grown icy as it joins up with the Shenandoah. Miss Jenny knows better than to let herself need, a woman whose best skill is living like a mouse inside the floorboards. But the night is cold. She can't stop rattling and stands too close to the fire.

See Jenny leaning in, like she's about to hug the flames. Notice the way her skirt catches, the sparks leaping onto worn wool threads. Hear the way she howls, poor Jenny, making such a sound. Flames claim the whole of her body, like a cruel lover and then some, every part of her gone red. She runs in the direction of the station, her cries more mangled with every step, her body becoming one long flame as the train rounds the bend with the hard, lonesome cry of its whistle. The conductor can't stop, can't do a thing but close his eyes as the little bonfire on the tracks is torn apart, sending Jenny to Kingdom Come. Except that Jenny never really leaves. She's still there in Harpers Ferry. No longer a mouse. No longer offering up every last crumb. No longer shivering or cold, Miss Jenny runs screaming along the tracks, finally and forever giving the world some of how she feels.

But we ghosts are not just South—though a ghost does hold on good and tight down here. So does Lydia, up in Skagway Bay, working her room at the Red Onion Saloon. Skagway, Alaska, a stopover for men on their way to the Yukon Territory and the goldfields up there. Men walk into the Red Onion, all eyes and torn fingers, requiring drinks and places to rest their heads. A whorehouse in a prospecting town—did Lydia have even an hour to be soft?

She did what she could, lying with any and all—dreamers and thieves—whichever hand came first with the dollar. How big they talked as they worked themselves up, filling every part of Lydia with hopes and well-intentioned lies, telling of the treasure they'd bring on their way back south—worse than the constant chug of their bodies, the gold talk and the promises. What men will say in the seconds leading up, what goodwill will fly from half-quivered mouths.

With such knowledge, Lydia might have turned philosopher in another place and time. But in Skagway, there's only gold-fevered rush. There are only the minutes between men, time spent managing other girls and contemplation of various routes back home. So many days, and none of them her own.

Only now does Lydia finally linger, pausing before windows and watering sometimes the plants. Over a century later, but still she does not tire of her own thoughts, the decadence of solitude. She takes her time floating down the hall, sometimes donning her old form like a favorite dress, trailing her overworked perfume as she passes, the saunter of leg and ass following her own rhythm, the movement of the body finally and forever for Lydia's pleasure alone.

There are others, of course. The Ozark Madonna wandering the ridges of southern Missouri, her baby in her arms. The girl on Highway 365, hitching rides from Little Rock to Pine Bluff. The Dancing Woman of Trollwood Park in Fargo. The child at the Orpheum Theatre in Memphis, dead one hundred years but still enjoying the shows. The Indian Maiden of Lake Waha, Idaho. Resurrection Mary in Chicago, Slag Pile Annie in Pittsburgh, the ghost of Queen Esther of the Iroquois. More ghosts than one can count. Flickering here and there, flaunting and haunting, walking halls and highways and forest paths. In every state, in every cut and color of dress—even and especially blue, and speaking of blue, they say in old Savannah to paint your porch ceiling the color of the sky so we ghosts can't get through. Ah, but we do. We do.

All of us are coming through. Carrying with us words held under the tongue for so many years—a thousand flocks of starlings flapping free, grazing the heads of the living as we push past, turning over rivers and houses, swooping into cottonwoods until every branch is blackened. Nothing like losing the body to better see the woman. The truest thing on earth is fear. The one thing that doesn't lie, a chill settling into the spine.

Here we come, mouths open, hands wide.

Can you feel it, the press of us just now against your flesh?

Tigers die and leave their skins;

people die and leave their names.

— JAPANESE PROVERB

SOME NAMES AND
WHAT THEY MEAN

Carmen. A Spanish form of *Carmel*, from the Hebrew for *garden*, as in Our Lady of Mount Carmel Church on Ontario Street, where angels skitter along the dome over the altar, the building between my neighborhood and the west side, where Carmen lived. Carmel. A name that sounds like smooth buttered candy. A name that can also mean *song*, as in a sweet, sad lullaby, an evening hymn, or the steady chant of prayer. Carmen. A name used mainly by Catholics, which is fitting perhaps because it was Catholic girls and their mothers who came to think of Carmen most.

November 1971. Two boys riding their bikes along the rural road thought they'd come upon a doll broken in the ditch. Bare except for a sweater and the socks and sneakers still on her feet, Carmen's body was splayed along the roadside as if tossed from a moving car, like a spent cigarette or a half-eaten apple.

Her body was returned to the city, to Saints Peter and Paul Church, where she was prayed over in Spanish (*Señor ten piedad*), set into a casket, anointed with incense, and placed in the ground. It snowed that day, people remarked. Later they will make similar statements as other bodies are carried from churches, reports of roses blooming in winter, a singular tear dried on the girl's cheek—such details become signs of the divine, a whiff of mystery shrouding the reality of a child's body left like rubble along the roadside.

27

But the body does not always stay in the ground. This one rises before me, a girl named for a garden, so that I see her: a dark-haired child with large brown eyes sent to a pharmacy in the Bull's Head neighborhood, where she lives. Her baby sister is sick—their father left years before, so her mother sends Carmen out for medicine. The girl, who is used to such errands, drops off the prescription like she's told, and in the time it takes the pharmacist to measure liquid into the bottle, a car pulls up along West Main Street. Like Hades, he is Death himself as the driver gathers Carmen into his chariot and heads west.

Incredibly, Carmen escapes. Naked from the waist down, the girl runs along Interstate 490, facing rush-hour traffic, arms flailing. She screams—Spanish is the language she knows best, so she probably screams, *Ayúdame*, or cries out for her *Mami*—but no matter what comes from her mouth or how loudly, everything in her small body working toward the sound, not one car among the hundreds zooming past slows down. No one stops at the next exit to find a pay phone and alert the police. No telephone calls are made once the commuters reach their homes. 5:30 p.m. Windows are rolled tight against the cold. Cars speed along the highway after a long day at work, so many meetings and phone calls, pressure built up from unreasonable demands, clients, and bosses—the drivers grip their steering wheels and look away, even as the child runs toward them, the green pants and long red coat she'd worn only an hour before already torn from her body. They look away, telling themselves that someone else will stop, that someone else will tend to the girl, or better yet, that the man backing up his car in her direction will settle the matter.

Wanda. From the Old German for *Wend*, referring to the Slavic peoples of eastern Europe, the name eventually came to mean *wanderer*. Appropriate for the one who'd gone missing from Avenue D. Wanda attended School No. 8, where she worked hard and was well liked, though she'd missed fifty-seven days already by April that year. She was there for picture day, at least, blue-eyed and freckled, a red-headed pixie smiling brightly into the camera.

According to Polish legend, a princess called Wanda became queen after her father's death. Brave beyond her years, Wanda threw herself into the Vistula River to avoid marriage and the surrender of Polish lands to her German suitor. Like her legendary namesake, Wanda Walkowicz was older than her eleven years and took charge at home, running errands and babysitting for her sisters, which may explain all the days missed from school. Like the father of the Polish princess, Wanda's father had died when she was young.

In early April, Wanda is sent out for groceries, and the next day her body, still in a blue-and-white checked dress, is found lying face down near a rest area in the nearby town of Webster. But first, she's a child facing a chilly day as she heads toward the neighborhood store. Not just bread and milk but diapers too. Cans of pet food and tuna fish. Cupcakes. A heavy bag, a rainy day. It's a tough neighborhood, but Wanda is, by all accounts, a firecracker. But no matter how big she might feel, she's all of sixty-five pounds and struggles to carry the overpacked bag down Conkey Avenue, leaning against walls and fence posts to get her bearings as she walks home in the cold drizzle. A girl walking home in the rain. It's the last way anyone saw her and the way she appears to me now—a child in a blue dress trying her best to hold on to more than she can carry.

There were other crimes, of course. Residents of any midsized city grow used to such things, come to expect them even—though it seems to me now that our city had more than its share, including the man who pulled young women into nearby garages to rape them. The Garage Rapist caused a buzz in the early seventies and provided another reason for girls and women to move more carefully along Rochester streets. But the murders of Carmen and Wanda were something else—two girls plucked from close to home. Seventeen months after Carmen's body was put into the earth at Holy Sepulchre, eleven-year old Wanda Walkowicz was laid in the same ground. There were other similarities. Both were Catholic; both were children of single mothers. Both were named with double initials; their bodies were found in towns bearing the same letter—Carmen Colon's body was left in Churchville, Wanda Walkowicz's in Webster. Like something out of Agatha Christie, except the murders were committed in the unrelenting gray of western New York instead of the quaint patchwork of the English countryside.

The city bristled under the brutality. Parents—especially single mothers—took extra care, but even then, after a few months, when no new bodies were discovered, the mothers began to relax, allowing things to slip back to normal, shaking their heads at the sad mystery of those girls, even as they called to their daughters, pushed a few dollars into their hands, and sent them around the corner for bread and milk.

Sonja. My own name bears no reference to the Virgin, is not as openly devotional as *Mary*, not as pure or hallowed as *Lily*. But when was my mother ever consistently religious? To her, religion was like macramé or painting with oils, activities in which she was either wholly engaged or completely uninvolved, depending on resources, competing distractions, and overall frame of mind. She may have been an erratic Catholic, but she was a committed and vigorous namer of things, and for my middle name, she chose Alena, diminutive of Helen, meaning bright, used by Saints Helena in Constantinople and Elen in Wales, patrons of difficult marriages and British road builders, respectively. *Sonja* itself is a name steeped in faith, though I'm not sure my mother ever knew it, am not sure what led her to choose it in an era of feathery-sounding Wendys, Heathers, and Hollys.

Sonja. The Slavic form of *Sophia*, as in the early Italian martyr and saint. Mother to three girls, Sophia named her daughters for the virtues, Faith, Hope, and Love—a long-standing tradition, the naming of babies for traits one hopes they'll embody. When Sophia came under fire by the Romans for her Christianity, the widow held fast to her faith—even as her girls were taken from her one at a time, tortured, and killed. The grieving Sophia buried their bodies and remained by their graves until she herself died and was placed in the same ground.

Sophia. From the Greek for *wisdom*, another virtue, and as a child, at least, I was a wise thing. While I could not make sense of details and was spared some of the worst, I noticed the strange turn of electricity in the air, the hushed talk of bodies and killers, and felt the reverberations of the sound no one wanted to hear but which became embedded in every brick and shingle of the city, the calls of a child running alone along the highway.

Like those of Carmen and Wanda, my family consisted of a single mother and six kids who followed her movements like a swarm of undersized shadows. We were Catholic and lived in parts of the city from which others had fled. I don't remember being especially afraid, but then, when you live long enough in any condition, you hardly notice the clenched jaw or the bend of the oversucked thumb. In kindergarten, I practiced my letters while imagining places I might hide, working out how quickly I might push my body into a kitchen cupboard or the cool, dark space under a bed.

Don't talk to strangers. Avoid those who call from cars. Schoolteachers and newscasters and mothers said this. Did they specifically mention men, or was it implied by the way we looked to the sidewalk when one passed, the way men were nearly strangers in that place of women and children? There might be a random husband or a stray boyfriend, of course, but men were most often spoken of in past tense, and when present, they were fleeting figures, deep-voiced specters sitting on porch steps, taking long drags from cigarettes and flicking away ashes as they came in and out of our lives. Mothers might be unpredictable, and boys should be careful when sprinting across busy streets and playing with sticks, but men were ghosts at best and hunters at worst, and girls were the equivalent of deer in winter and must be cautious, taking pains to tread lightly while keeping voices lowered, doing whatever possible to avoid attracting attention.

Michelle. French and feminine. A form of Michael, from the Hebrew for *Who is like God?* The name itself a question. Michelle is from my neighborhood. Her funeral takes place at Corpus Christi, where we attend church and school. Five years after her burial at Holy Sepulchre, my mother and her children will move onto a street just one over from where Michelle lived, making a home of a dead end parallel to the one that had been hers.

On a late November day in 1973, Michelle walks home from No. 33

School in her purple coat and knee-high boots. She's been kept after school for something she hasn't done. The target of bullies, the soft child walks down Webster Avenue, though it's unclear where the eleven-year-old is headed as the car slows—there are reports she cut through Goodman Plaza on the way home to retrieve a purse her mother had left at a store. Is she thinking of getting home, her mother's purse, or something else as the car slows? Does he call her pretty, the man at the wheel? Does he say, *My God, now here's a sight for sore eyes*, to the girl whose father has left, whose peers are known to be cruel? Either way, the window comes down, revealing the face of someone she knows or a persuasive stranger, a man who says, *Hop in*, and dutiful child, she does as she's told, and two days later, Michelle Maenza's body is found along the roadside in the rural town of Macedon.

Three girls. Taken from the places they knew best. Kidnapped and killed. And something else. Something worse than death. Something I don't yet understand but which settles heavy under my skin. The television news reports that two of the girls were found with food in their bellies, including Michelle. He'd fed them, possibly lured them with the promise of a treat. Poor girls are hungry girls. I was named for the Greek word for wisdom and understood this. *Who is like God?* I did not consider such questions—if I allowed myself inquiries, it was over the matter of mouths, pink as new roses, opening like fishes' before the hook.

Two decades later. Graduate school. Against the odds, I've made it out of the neighborhood, but my escape is so new I'm aware of myself primarily as an imposter, even in classes where our desks are set into circles, as if we are friends. In education classes, we talk gender—or perhaps this particular class is organized around gender—I only recall the question the professor asks: *How many here have been sexually harassed?*

Hands fly up, all except those of the one or two men and my own, which remain folded on my lap, making my silence the loudest thing in the room. The teacher turns my way: *What about you, not even once?*

I cannot speak. Not because of my rising ambivalence toward classroom discussions but because the question asks about harassment as if it is a concrete thing, a one-time event—as if fear and being female in the world had a beginning and an end, as if it were outlined in black and could be colored in with crayons, as if I might lift a page, show it to the professor, and have her understand. Should I mention my old neighborhood, where girls learned to wake early to avoid the feel of so many eyes? Even before our periods came, we were bodies. We had names, and those who knew us spoke them—prettily sometimes and other times like curses—but we were bodies, first and last. How to explain the way the posture sinks from so much time spent folding the body inward, and the permanent bend of the head turned down, so that even when the girl escapes, she remains the child sent to the store for bread and milk, her body remarked upon like the groceries in her bag, *Mmm, mmm, mm—hot damn* and *good enough to eat.*

But the professor is waiting so I try to isolate incidents—the boss, the boyfriend, the man on the street. These are the stories she wants, but the past spills its shadows and runs together—and even as I wade through a tangle of memory, I'm aware that twenty years after the Alphabet Killer, there's another killer at work in our city, snagging grown women, raping and strangling, leaving their bodies in river gorges and creeks, some of the bodies tattooed with the cut of his teeth. I stare into space, old threats mingling with new, and cannot separate out the threads—so dumb the look on my face, the teacher eventually takes pity and moves on.

What would have happened—it's cruel to imagine—but what would have happened if Michelle and Carmen and Wanda had lived? I never met them but was of them. Girls living in homes with sisters and sometimes brothers, but always a mother. Girls sent to the store and asked to carry bags they could barely manage—not because their mothers were cold but because their hands too were full. Girls no one seemed to expect much from. Girls sitting in classes trying to answer whether they'd ever been harassed, struggling the way one must struggle to describe the feel of water when she's never lived anywhere but rivers and streams. I look into their photographs, the Peter Pan collars, crooked bangs, and all that's held behind the eyes, and recognize them the way the body knows the push of blood through the veins.

Louise. From the Old German for *famous warrior*. My mother's name. Fitting because of the way she uses a hammer to sink nails into the window frames on the first floor. It's a simple house, shingles repainted gold; my mother traded our dining-room furniture to pay for the paint job. The man who does the painting looks into the windows. Five of us girls. The man across the street points a telescope into our bedrooms. A feast for the eyes. But these are temporary distractions. The paint job will be done in a summer. The man with the telescope will be removed by the police after beating his wife once too often. Right now, it's something else, and my mother holds a hammer in one hand and several long nails in the other.

The local community center trains mothers to secure their windows. A man's been entering homes, raping teenage girls. The Northeast Rapist, he's called, and here we are, in the Northeast accompanied by the sound of the hammering, my mother leaning her short body into the job, bandana keeping the hair out of her face as she pounds into the window frame. We shake our heads as she works. Wasn't it just a few years ago that we slept on the front porch? Was the neighborhood less dangerous then, or had a few years without a named enemy made us reckless? Perhaps enough time had elapsed between the Alphabet Killer and the Northeast Rapist, years before Shawcross began to leave a trail of bodies in local ravines, years after the Garage Rapist put a gun to his own head.

What nights they were on the porch. All talk and dreaming and starlight. We zipped our sleeping bags together into a massive cushioned square, making a communal bed, sisters and friends, a bunch of girls, laughing until we fell asleep. All that soft skin and glossy hair lying on porch slats like pies set to cool on the windowsill.

Desiree: From the French, meaning desired. Is there a similar name for boys, or are girls alone named as objects of desire? Desire itself is not such a bad name. It is active, at least, a verb, a more muscular form of want and how much I want to go back to 1971. To 490 West, where commuters look straight ahead, driving as fast as they can and shutting their eyes and ears to the child running half-naked along the highway, like I might have done. But not now. Now I know better and slow my car as I look out the window at the maples losing their leaves, their bare branches becoming shadow in the last bit of light. There she is, our girl. I stop and open the door, using the little Spanish I know to soothe her, *Está bien, mi chica, it's okay ahora.*

She's a trusting girl, even after so many years. Once she's buckled in and caught hold of her breath, we forget everything we've left behind and merge onto the New York State Thruway toward Buffalo and north to the falls. A cold day, but she hasn't ever been to Niagara Falls and smiles as I describe the tumble of water, the blue-green rush, the wash of light. She's warm now, Carmen; her clothes have found their way back to her body, soft, fine things—and just like that, we understand that we can't yet go to the falls, that it will no longer do to be afraid. I turn the car and double-back along the thruway—heading east, back to the city and Conkey Avenue, stopping for another girl, this one with eyes so blue they almost hurt. We help her into the car, relieve her of the grocery bag falling apart in her hands. A jolt of energy, she chatters as we push toward Goodman Plaza, where we spot a dark-haired girl stepping over a broken bottle near a vacant lot on Ackerman Street. We call out, and she sees us and knows we are friends, and all of us, separated by the years and a few city streets, strangers and sisters, decide it's time for new names, trading in those of the quiet, the saintly, and the small, for something brand new.

We turn onto Clifford Avenue and pass Savoia's Bakery, which makes me think of weddings and cookie trays and the name of my friend's Italian grandmother.

Fortunata, I say out loud, *a name that means lucky.*

The girls giggle and there's the slightest shuffle of breath before one of them offers another name:

Valentina, from the Latin, meaning brave and strong.

The others join in: *Cordelia, for heart, a legendary queen of the Britons. Mapiya, a Sioux name meaning sky. Kendra, from the Welsh, meaning champion. Farren, from the English for adventurous. Sekhmet, from the old Egyptian, for she who is powerful.*

We continue, spurred on by the feel of such names in our mouths:

Celosia, aflame.

Olinda, wild fig.

Nabhitha, fearless.

The last few are tempting, as we consider who we might become, trying each one out before staking claim on those we like best.

Once we've decided and have rechristened ourselves with new names—the power of such a thing—all that's left is the road and the question of where we'd most like to go. But not yet. A whisper now, from the back seat, a voice so quiet I barely hear—one of the girls is still weighing her options, saying a few more names and wavering, but at last she speaks a final name:

Aisha, comes the voice, strong now and clear, *from the Arabic, meaning "she who lives."*

Mary Doyle is a recently discovered Irish ancestor hiding out in a family of French Canadians. While attempting to research the woman who left County Mayo in 1899, I quickly realized that she was only one in a tide of Mary Doyles leaving Ireland in the nineteenth century. Ireland had bled people for generations, but from the mid-nineteenth century to 1925, its population was halved, with more people dying or leaving than staying behind. With no prospect for jobs or husbands, young Irish women boarded westbound ships in droves.

A THOUSAND
MARY DOYLES

There she is, Mary Doyle, and another right beside her. Head turned for one last view of land before the Cork coastline slips out of sight. Dishwater strands pushed behind her ears, yellow curls pulled up under a hat, dark frizz flying in the wind. She is seventeen. She is twenty-two. She is just yesterday turned twenty-nine. Look at her now, studying the sky in place of crying, trying to remember what everyone has said, begging Mary-the-most-holy-mother-of-God they might make it across the ocean alive.

She leaves behind her favorite cow and the kitchen garden she's been fighting for years. She leaves behind her mother's grave, her sister's face, and her Uncle Timmo's way with the plow. She leaves behind the traveling priest, the Sunday Masses, and the words to every song she knows, *My apple tree, my brightness*, and *Oh ro, soon shall I see them*, the pretty laments and the keening, and Mr. Byrne with the tin whistle, and here it comes now, her father's hand, swollen and cracked as it is, the way he held it to her, her father's hand, soft as old cloth against her cheek.

She leaves behind the big house on the hill and the broken buggy leaning against Coughlan's cottage. Will it oh will it ever get fixed? And the marsh violet and the burnet rose and the blackthorn too sometimes, the patchwork of fields, and the baby Lizzie with her dark eyes and funny ways—what will the little one be like as she grows? And the abbey, of course, what times they had there, the slick moss and cold stone, and her best friend, Birdy, who swears upon her life she will write, but both girls know how these things go, a few long letters at first, the distance between them widening as the world settles into the spaces made by those who leave, until words are folded less often into envelopes, because if there's one thing everyone knows, it's that when someone leaves Ballyhaunis, sure enough, she's gone for good.

Mary Doyle.

Come from Moycullen from Westmeath and Usher's Quay. Come from Poulnamuck, Gweesalia, and Tourmakeady. From Clongeen, Collooney, and Cahermacrea. From Kilkelly and Kilmeena, Ballina and Bonniconlon. From Portlaoise, Mountshannon, and Roscommon. From Donoughmore, Dún Laoghaire, and Drogheda.

That one there with the reddish hair, the tall one with the overproud back, the one gone flat against the rail, trying her best to hide the sight of a broken shoe under her trunk, fan of fingers placed on her brow. That one. And that one. Then again that one too. Sailed in 1851. Sailed in 1847. Left from Queenstown in 1869. Doing what she must in order to survive.

See her now, stepping from the gangway, swaying a bit as her feet reach solid land. That's her there, scanning the crowd for the sight of a familiar face. And here we are. We can't call out, but we can at least see her, every girl bound for Boston, New York, and the Upper Saint Lawrence. We can't call out, but we can look for a moment in her direction to see what might be found in her face, for she belongs to all of us, does our girl, Mary Doyle.

Alice Mitchell met Freda Ward at the Higbee School for Girls in the late 1880s, in Memphis. The girls became fast friends, and eventually more than friends. They hatched a plan to elope, with Alice posing as a man, but were caught and forbidden to see each other. The crime that followed shocked the nation, which turned its eyes to Memphis for details not only of the murder but of the strange desire Alice confessed of wanting to marry another girl.

MAD LOVE
THE BALLAD OF
FRED AND ALLIE

The sin was not so much the taking of the throat as the wanting of it in the first place. And what a fine throat it was, the way it captured those who saw it, men loitering at the Customs House, boys down by the river stretching their necks to catch a glimpse, the entire nation eventually taking note. But in the beginning it was only Alice, the first to be lassoed by Miss Freda's charms.

It must have been the way she walked into the music room at Miss Higbee's School for Young Ladies. Only the best girls came to Miss Higbee's School, from the best families in Memphis—not always the first families, mind, those with places at the Cotton Exchange on Front Street, but always from the most respectable families, which is how Freda's people were set, a touch heavier on the respectability than the money. But my God, how that girl could twirl her hips like the women selling their wares down on Pontotoc, laughing like a child before breaking into song. And the voice. Miss Freda could catch a river of fish with her singing, with a finger hooked in the lips between songs, walking haughty and making fun when the Mistress wasn't looking. Frederica Ward. Known as Freda or Freddie, but mostly just Fred. Brown eyes. Body like a new branch in spring, thin but coming together with new growth. Like the petals of a magnolia, Fred Ward's body, all silk white and cupping.

The brick building on the corner of Beale and Jessamine is shaded from the afternoon sun by a stand of slender elms; all seventeen of its classrooms provided wide, cool spaces for girls of a certain means with lessons in art, literature, Latin, and Greek. With French lessons, a music room, and even a governess named Miss Aurelia Lane; how could the girls not emerge from Miss Higbee's School more charming than when they'd entered? All that poetry and music in their heads, the pink roses climbing outside the windows. Three hundred of the best girls in Memphis attended the school in 1890, among them Alice Mitchell and Fred Ward.

All they did at first was look. Just look. Something moving in Alice while following the hair gathered at Fred's neck, the turns of the lone dark curl tucked behind the ear, and yes, the throat, as if made of marble. Memphis had never seen a fine child, and she knew it, Fred did, piling that hair and running a finger along her mouth as she swallowed, smiling all the while, smiling at her dearest friends, including Alice, who replied in kind. Until it was only Alice. The girls talked in the code they'd devised, a universe unto themselves, using no words, but saying everything with the work of their mouths.

"How I love thee; none can know."

Letter from Alice Mitchell to Freda Ward, 1891

The girls could not have been more different. Fred embraced music and drama and flitted from room to room, while Alice's passions centered on baseball and horses. Despite their differences, they became fast friends, and in at least one way were a perfect match; Alice adored Fred, who, in turn, demonstrated great skill at being adored. They had pet names: Fred called Alice "Sweetheart," and Alice called Fred "Petty Sing."

The girls twined round each other in the hammock for hours, held hands, and spent so much time in each other's clutches that, at times, friends called them disgusting. But these complaints were launched lightly; such relationships were not only accepted at the Higbee School but were encouraged by society as they kept the girls from ruining themselves with men before marriage. Neither Allie nor Fred were allowed much interaction with boys or the world outside home and school without strict supervision. But with each other, they found nearly limitless freedom.

"Sing, I have a rose for you; if it is not withered by the next time I see you, I will give it to you. I have been trying to get one for a long time. It beats all other roses."

Letter from Alice Mitchell to Freda Ward, 1891

But good God in heaven, what but what was up in Golddust, Tennessee?

Nothing but mud fields and shacks set onto stilts and row after row of cotton. Fred's father had changed his business to planting and moved them all upriver, Fred, along with her sisters and brother-in-law. And just like that, two who could not be untwined from each other were pulled apart.

Golddust was a romantic enough name. Fred may have even tried to make it sound pretty in her letters to Alice, writing of horned larks or the stand of pecan trees just outside her window, but Alice's daddy would have been up that way and told Alice there was nothing in Golddust but mud. Mud and cotton. But if he tried to console his daughter with such images, Alice did not oblige. The girl wouldn't touch a thing on her plate. No matter how her Mama and Cook begged, the reality of Golddust itself had become a cake of dirt on her tongue.

Golddust was all Alice could think of, the place that held what she most wanted to hold. It maddened her to think of Fred with her pretty dresses and feathered caps, sitting in a stilted shack sixty miles upriver. Fred could still come to visit Memphis, of course, but there would be no more regular dances at the social club, no more nights together at

Miss Higbee's School. Alice had only memories of times they'd sneaked away to stare at the stars, with the moon guiding them. Surely there were other memories, secrets held tight between the girls. Either way, there was nothing to do but stand at the levee and look across the river to Arkansas, waiting for steamers traveling between Saint Louis and New Orleans to carry their letters from Memphis to Golddust and back again.

✦

Fred was miserable, too, without Allie, or at least she laid such claims. Letters from Golddust became confessions of flirtations with young men coupled with promises of fidelity to Alice, whose anxieties multiplied with each new letter:

Fred, do you love me one-half as much as you did the first winter? I believe you loved me truer than you ever did. You didn't fall in love with every boy that talked sweet to you then. Sweet one, you have done me mean, but I love you still with all your faults.

Yes, Fred replied, she did love Alice still: *Sweet love, you know that I love you better than anyone in the wide world. I want to be with you all the time, for I more than love you. Good-bye until tomorrow.—Sing*

There were visits, weeks when Alice boarded the steamship to Golddust, times Fred visited the Mitchell home in Memphis. Satisfying exchanges evidently, so satisfying that by late July 1891, the newly seventeen-year-old Fred began to wear the gift of jewelry sent up from Memphis by her eighteen-year-old beloved.

✦

"I received the ring all
ok. Sweetheart, you know I want to marry you;
I don't only want to, but am going to marry you."
Letter from Freda Ward to Alice Mitchell, 1891

✦

Something must have threatened to spill from Alice—what she must have felt!—to have secured such a promise from her love. At heart, they might have known how hopeless their engagement, and perhaps it was this that led them to act too quickly—though given the prospect of two women eloping in 1891, there was no particular time that would have improved their chances. Such a marriage was impossible, but what is impossibility in the face of love?

They did what they could and hatched a plan: Fred would take the steamship *Rosa Lee* from Golddust to Memphis, where Alice would be waiting. Fred might not recognize Alice straightaway, for she might already be wearing trousers and a Norfolk jacket, hair set under a bowler hat, answering only to the name of Mr. Alvin Mitchell. The girls knew enough to know that one of them would have to pass for a man if they were to marry, and with her boyish inclinations, Alice was the natural choice.

They might have heard of women posing as men at Miss Higbee's School, whispering in the dormitory, giggling in the corners of the drawing studio. Their parents had lived through the Civil War, and the girls may have heard stories of women who dressed as men to fight, women such as Mollie Bean and Cathay Williams. Fred, who'd delighted in the theater, would have known of Viola posing as Cesario in Shakespeare's *Twelfth Night* and Portia in *The Merchant of Venice*. With no boys to fill the roles, the girls probably even played male parts during plays at the Higbee School.

However the idea arrived, it came to them strong and sure, so that the girls had no trouble imagining Alice in trousers and short hair. It became their ticket to freedom, Alice's manning up, the thing to allow them to say good-bye to Memphis and board the steamer, holding hands and heading north, to Saint Louis, where they'd disembark and say, *I do*. A date was set for late July, and what thoughts the girls must have had as the magnolia-laden days of June slipped away and July finally approached.

The heat hangs heavy along the lower Mississippi River in summer. The girls would have wiped their brows as they packed their cases, one in Memphis, the other upriver, then sat waiting, their thoughts racing to the backbeat of crickets, the whir of cicadas. How short every breath, how humid the air. The scent of jasmine wafting from verandas, the air thickening as evening arrived, expectant as a coming storm.

This was the moment, the point at which they were still girls, half-drunk on possibility, all jittery and looking forward, hearts flung open foolish and wide.

Miss Allie Mitchell,

Ere now you must fully realize that your supposed well laid plans to take Fred away have all gone awry. You should have taken into consideration that Fred had a sister watching over her who had good eyes and plenty of common sense. . . . I return your "engagement ring" as you called it, and all else that I know of your having sent Fred.

Letter from Mrs. W. H. Volkmar, August 1, 1891

They were caught. Of course, they were caught.

If their friendship seemed more affectionate than usual, it was tolerated. Even when the girls were separated, no one thought of them as anything but the usual chums until the night they packed their bags and tried to insert themselves into the wider world without the permission of fathers, brothers, or husbands.

What did girls dream of in 1891? Perhaps the very idea of dreaming of anything other than lives as wives and mothers was a radical act. In this way, Fred and Alice were renegades of the highest order.

It's said that Fred dreamed of the stage, an impossibility for girls of her class, whose wedding day with its orange blossoms and stacked cake would be the most drama one could expect. But she dreamed of the stage anyway, the sway of glittered hemlines, the never-ending change of costumes, the beauty of art in motion, a northern city, far from the sand and muck of Golddust, far from snarls of men baling cotton, far from the slump of women grown tired with waiting.

As for her dreams, Allie seems to have wanted most of all the sight of Fred in a bridal dress, a tree to climb perhaps, a shared bed, night after night, the sound of horses galloping in a nearby field, the freedom of running, and trousers and no one telling her what to do.

But it was not to be. Fred's brother-in-law saw a light on in her room late at night, found her packed and waiting, and stopped her from leaving Golddust with a Winchester in his hand. Did she protest when her sister and brother-in-law discovered her plan? All those fields cracked dry in the summer, the cotton starting to open, miles of white dabs in all directions but the river? What of Alice sitting downriver? Where did she fix her eyes as she waited? How many stars in the sky that night? How many times did Alice retrace the contours of the past, remembering them together under the cloak of night sky as she waited for the sight of Fred—oh would oh would oh would her one true love come?

"Sing, I don't do a thing but have the blues all the time."

Alice Mitchell to Freda Ward, 1891

The blues were nothing new to Memphis. W. C. Handy hadn't yet written "The Memphis Blues," but by the 1890s, there was already plenty of sad singing on Beale Street. Freed people had come from all parts of the Deep South to the shops and storefronts along Union and Beale. And fields. It was the Delta, after all. Cotton was still king, baled and stacked by the river, as it had always been, graded and sold in the same places where, a few decades prior, human cargo had also been unloaded. Buggies and mules shuddered beside the levee while men made deals along the riverfront and streetcars screeched through packed streets, competing with the sounds of the new railroad bridge going up over the Mississippi.

No, Handy hadn't yet written his famous song, but Memphis had already endured its share of the blues. The city had been broken by yellow fever epidemics, the last of which hit in 1878; it claimed so many lives that Memphis collapsed under the weight of its losses and nearly did not recover.

By 1890, the city was booming again, but even as the girls sat studying elocution and Latin at Miss Higbee's School, it was not uncommon for violence to erupt in the streets surrounding them. Alice and Fred would have grown up with stories of the saffron-colored skin of those lost to the fever. They would have heard accounts of black men hanging from trees, would have absorbed the sounds of the lonesome singing on Beale, the strumming of strings. Yes, even those girls at Miss Higbee's, wrapped in their ruffles and lace collars, would have understood what it meant to have the blues.

When Alice was cut off from Fred and the engagement ring returned, she threatened to kill herself with laudanum. She cried to her mama and told her troubles to Cook in the kitchen, saying her heart was caving in on itself. But no one seemed to understand, especially not Cook, who only replied that at least it was only love she lost, and "nothin' so bad as being poor."

No one could rouse Alice. She continued to write to Fred but received no response. No matter how those around her tried, Alice refused to budge from her grief, becoming so thin that her dresses began to float about her as summer moved into fall. The crape myrtles lost their flowers, the water oaks dropped their acorns, and even the holiday season, with its firecrackers and gunshots, did nothing to revive Alice. No, it seemed Alice could not bring herself to care about a thing. Until her true love returned to town.

A freeze settled on Memphis that winter, a rarity in the part of the state that leans upon the Mississippi Delta with both its knees. Snow and ice had gripped the city for weeks, and when, finally, the weather relented enough to allow travel, Alice took a buggy out. She asked her friend Lillie to join her, and together they clopped up and down the streets near their homes, including Madison, where they passed the Widow Kimbrough's house, and imagine Alice's surprise when through the window she spied Fred!

After absorbing the raw shock of seeing her beloved's face, after keeping herself from clawing through the window just to touch it, Alice must have pulled back and taken stock. She would have smarted at seeing Fred come to town without so much as a word. As if Alice no longer mattered. As if Miss Freda Ward could puff her sweetness all over Memphis and think Alice would not find out. The world was in ruins, with Fred so close by and never once coming to call. When she returned home to the small box of special things she kept, the one she liked so much to mull over, she would have found the ring Fred had worn when she promised marriage. How Alice must have stared at that small band, setting it into her own hand, pushing her finger over its cold surface, going round and round, thinking of what to do.

In January 1892, snow fell as the three girls walked past the Customs House toward the steamship docked at the landing. Fred, her sister, and a friend were headed back to Golddust; the girls shivered as they huddled together and crossed toward the levee, none of them noticing the buggy trailing them.

Alice, with her friend Lillie once again beside her, followed the trio toward Front Street, guiding the buggy in their shadow. Alice said by way of explanation as she jumped out into the street, *Fred winked at me, Lillie, she winked at me!*

Did Fred wink? Was she playing a game with Alice, teasing the girl who was dog-loyal in her affection? Or was the wink a lie, something Alice had only hoped to see? Something she wanted so badly that she actually did see? Either way, no one in Fred's party paid much mind to the fair-haired girl as she jumped from the carriage and ran up the stone path. None of them saw the wild look in her eyes until it was too late. No one understood just how serious she was until the razor was unfolded and in Alice's hand.

A MOST SHOCKING CRIME.

A MEMPHIS SOCIETY GIRL CUTS A FORMER FRIEND'S THROAT.

New York Times, January 26, 1892

A TRAGEDY EQUAL TO THE MOST MORBID IMAGININGS OF
MODERN FRENCH FICTION

Memphis Public Ledger, January 26, 1892

That Alice killed the one she loved best was never disputed. Lillie later testified to Alice's return to the buggy, the way she refused to wipe away the blood on her face because it had belonged to Fred, and how she'd only asked about the quickest way to kill herself. Alice herself admitted to the killing, saying she'd planned to cut her own throat as well but had been thrown off course when Fred's companions interfered.

In fact, the trial that captivated the nation was not for murder but for lunacy. Alice admitted her love for Fred in court, speaking of their plans to marry, her own idea to dress as a man and take a job to support them. She spoke of these things openly in 1892, in Memphis. And without a speck of shame.

The press descended. Public interest in the Memphis Girl Murder was such that the judge had his courtroom enlarged with a special stand for the press—the room was said to be the largest one in the city outside the local theaters. An apt comparison, since the room was jammed each day with men and women, black and white, craning their necks as the prosecution attempted to paint Alice as a cold-blooded killer, and given the way she'd cut a throat in broad daylight with witnesses and her own confession, it seemed a fair enough portrayal.

The defense's claim that Alice Mitchell was insane was supported by witnesses who spoke of her preference for sports and her skill at baseball. They testified that a sack of marbles was found in her room, described to the court the strange lack of dolls. One young man testified that Alice had once refused to dance with him at a picnic. Another claimed that when he called her a tomboy, Alice had not seemed to mind.

"A girl that thinks to assume the mask of a man, can shuffle off the baptismal name given her and take the name of Alvin J. Ward, take the place of a man and marry a woman—Your Honor knows there was madness at the bottom of that."

Colonel Gantt, testifying for the defense
"The Pity of It," Memphis Appeal Avalanche, February 26, 1892

THE APPEAL-AVALANCHE

WILL CONTAIN

FROM

DAY

TO

DAY

A

COMPLETE REPORT

OF THE PROGRESS

OF THE UNPARALLELED

MITCHELL-WARD-JOHNSON

GIRL MURDER TRIAL

IN ALL

ITS DETAILS,

FULLY ILLUSTRATED.

Memphis Appeal Avalanche, February 24, 1892

In the end, there were no surprises. Alice's love for Fred was considered more outrageous than the act of murder. She was found legally insane and committed to the State Insane Asylum in Bolivar on August 1, 1892—a year from the day she'd stood waiting for Fred to step from the *Rosa Lee*, a year from the day on which her prospects were shown to be as small as the mud-flat town where Fred sat crying sixty miles upriver.

Perhaps Alice was truly a lunatic and would have killed Fred anyway. Maybe something was loose in her head, so that even if they had made it to Saint Louis and she could coax a mustache from her face, the violence would have arisen. But who would have remembered it then, a killing between man and wife? No, it is only the fact of their shared girlhood that shocked the world. Nice girls from good families, so that people were left to wonder over those nights at Miss Higbee's School, the neck and the blade, the claims of love. What could they do with such a girl but send her to the madhouse? Alice perhaps stole one last look at the wide bend of the Mississippi before turning in her seat and leaning into her mama as the carriage headed east, away from the singing on Beale and the city Alice would never see again.

There goes that Alice Mitchell
With arms tightly bound down
For the crime she did in Memphis,
She's bound for Bolivar now.

Excerpt, "The Ballad of Alice Mitchell & Freddy Ward"
Collected by John Quincy Wolf, Wolf Folklore Collection, 1969

The ride east seems to have been gentle, given the circumstances, and those in the carriage complied when Alice asked to stop to say goodbye to Fred. They pulled up at Elmwood Cemetery on the way out of the town, likely stopping near the gate, taking whatever shade they could under oaks that had been standing longer than the cemetery itself. When they could go no longer by carriage, they would have disembarked and passed bald cypresses on foot, treading between limestone angels and stone anchors, the air filled with the sound of a train pulling coal from one side of the country to the other, until finally, Alice stood over the square of turned earth that had not yet settled back into the space over Freda Ward's body.

Did she hear Fred then? As she stood before the grave, did the sound of low and hard whistling give way to Fred's voice, a sound that must have been to Alice what the singing of birds is to the sky. And if she closed her eyes just then, was she back on Jessamine and Beale, where nothing was so true as the light coming through the windows of Miss Higbee's School, the sounds of hooves on the stones beneath the music room? Could she feel the heat of the other girls, their laughter and delight as Fred practiced her flirty walk? Did it seem for a moment as if they'd never left? And if she closed her eyes just right, might Alice allow herself to imagine that they'd boarded that boat to Saint Louis after all? That she stood not before a new grave but aboard a steamship, holding her love's hand, watching the levee disappear as they head north, the world opening wide before them.

Eleanor and Ananias Dare landed in present-day North Carolina as part of an attempt by Queen Elizabeth to establish a colony in North America in 1587. Eleanor gave birth to a daughter in Roanoke, and her father, who was the governor of the colony, left the settlement a few months later and returned to England to secure additional supplies. When he finally returned to the colony, everyone, including the baby Virginia, had vanished. A few letters carved into wood were the only trace of the 115 men, women, and children who became known as the Lost Colony.

DARE

I come to you mainly for your name. Your last name, of course.
Dare.

How much I'd like it for my own. But since we are to meet, I'm
inclined to skip the seduction of the second name and simply call you
Ginny. And I promise, child, as I parachute to your side with bits of
electric ink—I promise to be nothing like the one who left you, the one
who loaded up his daughter, belly already firm, though he could not be
sure they'd make it across the sea alive. Do you remember, Ginny, the
feel of ocean through the hull?

You were cargo, lifted with sacks of seed and root onto a ship of
unwashed men, bound for a place where the air was said to smell of
roses, where each was promised five hundred acres, but even in utero,
I'll bet you understood that the acres would be difficult, knew to expect
nothing more than wind and salt. Three boatloads of people asked to
make roses of bear grass and live oak. I swear, I am nothing like that,
Virginia. I'm nothing if not soft. And really, can it matter what I call
you? Can it matter the color of your eyes—whether, as I suspect, they
were the first of many blue coins flipped into the open pocket of the
New World? It is only the fact of your birth and the greater fact of your
disappearance that matter to the world. Your grandfather returned with
provisions three years later, on your birthday they say, and yes, clever
girl, you sense my cynicism through this mess of paper and time, be-

cause even as I make room for supposition, sentiments and superstition, I do not allow for such coincidences as birthday arrivals by wayward British grandpas—though it might be the one true thing, truer even than your eyes, so like the water off Hatteras. It's strange, I suppose, to be so peculiar about what I will and will not allow.

But this is what I do. I push myself into the air and hover over the windswept barrier islands, over tangled beaten beaches, to the string of green land wedged between the Banks and coastal Carolina, and when finally I find you, the weight of your body curled like a nautilus in my lap, we sit on a strip of sinking sand. Your hair smells of shellfish and juniper, your skin is browner than your mother would have seen fit, and the sound of your murmuring in my arms is like waves. I watch your eyes moving under closed lids. You're dreaming of scuppernong vines. You're imagining crabbing in the sound. Or else—because of the way I have just felt the flinch of your little finger—you're having that feeling again of falling. You are. But these words are only an exercise in possibility, recognition of the weight of even so small a child, and testament of my superficial devotion—for if your father's last name were Davis or Hightower in place of Dare, would I be here to cradle you on the page?

It's the name I wrap in buckskin and strands of Spanish moss; it's the idea of you I swaddle. Dare.

Virginia Dare.

1587. Mary, Queen of Scots, has been tried for treason and executed at the hand of her Protestant cousin; the loss of the English throne is a fresh ache for Catholics. Shakespeare is alive, though on unexplained hiatus. Walter Raleigh has been knighted for the first trip he organized to Roanoke, for tales and tobacco and Indians paraded before Queen Elizabeth's court. And so they set sail, your mother and father and grandfather among them, thinking of sisters seen for the last time, the beds they were born in, the sounds of villages they will no longer hear.

What do they speak of to pass the time? We know nothing of such things, for they recorded only the weather and replenishment of supplies. Your mother, a handful of women, and all those men—how they must move with care around each other, how they must learn to choose just the right word. All those people contained on ships, bound for spaces they'd never seen. How many swear to the sight of land before it ever comes? Is your mother sick with you? Does she freckle from so much time spent in the sun? Do they let themselves dream, or do they block out all but what's needed for survival? There are certain evenings, surely, the fat moon hanging overhead, when they allow themselves slippery talk, predicting the taste of feasts to come and speaking of trees that grow gold.

Eventually they hit land, make stops in the West Indies. They grow sick from green fruit given them in Saint Croix, gather orange saplings at Saint John, hunt swans in Caicos. Then the landing. Cape Fear. Hatteras. Roanoke. It's said they were bound for Chesapeake but were abandoned by their Portuguese captain. So it was Roanoke.

It is late July. The muscadines do not grow so well this year. Nor the corn. So your grandfather, colony leader, heads once again into the sea, saying he'll be right back, the sixteenth-century equivalent of a run to the corner store. But there's a war with Spain to keep him, and you're gone when he returns, which is the mystery but really no big surprise. Who, with mouth and eye, would not turn to some other source after three Christmases and Easters of scanning the horizon? After even a month of such waiting, everything must begin to look like a boat.

Fever might have taken you. Or starvation. Perhaps the Spaniards came north from Saint Augustine. But no, I see them clearly, pointed beards, stuck in Florida mud, hypnotized by flocks of flame-tipped birds, dipping and redipping their ladles into the Fountain of Youth. Some say your party headed north in search of Chesapeake. Others imagine a raid by natives, revenge taken for the murder of their chief the year before—but would someone strike down so little a girl, the palest child ever seen? New evidence says you were raided upon and taken as slaves.

Either way, I think of Tuscaroras with gray eyes and know that something of you survives beyond labels plastered to the sides of vanilla extract and canisters of tobacco. Like any child of America, you would have lost your Englishness first, a necessity, I think, trading in the silvery lilt for something more like tree bark, your new voice coiled like a water moccasin at the back of the throat.

Virginia. Virginia Dare.

How much I know without knowing. The way you learn to make salve of saliva and loblolly needles, can skin a deer in five minutes flat, give birth to four healthy boys. The way, on certain evenings, you hide in grass and dune, looking beyond the outer bank, not so much for the man you know will never come but for the color of the sky as it lets itself into the ocean, somehow like the memory of your mother's face. And isn't it true, Ginny, that nothing is hard forever, that even the press of memory eventually relents? So that I think you feel something opening inside you as each of your children, more golden than the last, is lifted from your body.

C R O A T O A N carved onto a fencepost.

C R O half-started on a tree. The name of a nearby tribe, those who may have saved or murdered you. And could they be blamed, the way your people took?

But that is all legend and myth. That is the part that ceases to matter. Whether or not you made it to Hatteras, soon labs will have analyzed DNA, bone fragment, and a little gold ring pulled from the sand. Soon all mystery will disappear. But what will that have to do with us, Ginny, and the way we have come together on the page—pulling strawberries by their green crowns, counting the leaves of the willow, finding a menagerie of animals hiding in the clouds?

It is only the thought of you, tiny girl, the fact of being born into bravery with or without your consent. *Virginia Dare.* Named for a virgin queen, baptized by hurricane, bug bite, and drought.

Your grandfather would have held you, would have swelled with pride at bringing forth the first English child in America, but while he sketched maps and made drawings of birds and trees and basket-bearing native girls, nothing was ever made of you.

And so, child of my lap, you remain untouched, tiny white fawn, bit of bone left lying along this stretch of beach—our first American ghost.

What becomes of the artists' models?

I am wondering if many of my readers have not stood before

a masterpiece of lovely sculpture or a remarkable painting

of a young girl . . . and asked themselves the questions,

"Where is she now, this model who was so beautiful?"

— AUDREY MUNSON

THE GODDESS OF
OGDENSBURG
A RISE AND FALL IN
SEVENTEEN POSES

POINT AIRY, 1991

This is how she comes to me, remembering again, eyes moving under her lids so that anyone can see she's dreaming. She weaves in and out of sleep, occasionally waking to the startled realization of where she is. Here again. Always here. Laughter streams tinny and hard from the television set. The sun is out, she notices as her eyes close, the ribbon of time bending so that she worries suddenly about protecting the milk of her skin—but there's the television laughter again and the reminder that she's at Point Airy. In a building on the river separating the northern portion of New York State from Canada. Wasn't it just yesterday 1919? How quickly a girl can rise and fall, silk and shine come in and out of a life before one can properly feel them. Those years in New York, a flash in the pan—a handful of red-letter days in the many blank pages of her life. Her lids flutter, lashes fringing the bluish half-moons under her eyes. The man with the camera stands before her—what's he saying now about her face—an angel, is it? But no. The image packs itself up and flits out the window, chased away by the sound of sobbing from the hall, the voice warbling and weathered but pleading as a child's as someone calls for his mother. One hundred years she's been alive. At Point Airy for most of them. The sound of singing drowns out the thought, her mother's voice, that old Irish song she sang while putting her to bed—the sound of singing and her mother, so close she can almost touch it until the squeak of shoes on overwaxed floors breaks the spell, and just like that, the only song is the soft gurgle of machinery and the insistent chirp of a sparrow flitting outside the window.

ROCHESTER, 1894

Audrey swings her arms as she walks toward Saint Patrick's Cathedral School. She's four years old, and the world around her is grander by the day. The Gilded Age. The first U.S. patent for an automobile has been granted. Biltmore, the Vanderbilt's lavish mansion in Asheville, nears completion. The nation hums to the sound of new motors, everyone looking forward. What better than the sight of a little girl whose dress flounces with ruffles, her braids finished off with oversized bows? The child is more than pretty, with her fair skin and dark hair waving just so. She collects smiles as she walks with her mother down Platt Street, becoming so used to the way people turn to have a look, it is perhaps strangest when they don't.

Her parents are in service in a home on East Avenue. It's this home —a mansion really, the likes of which are built by George Eastman and the other newly rich on Rochester's booming east side—that may put rhinestones and feathers into Kittie Munson's head. The world sizzles around her, but apart from the minks she removes from other women's backs, Kittie's daughter is her only treasure. Even when her husband leaves a few years later, Audrey continues to flower.

Audrey's parents have a mixed marriage from the start: Kittie is Irish and Catholic, while Edgar is a Protestant with a good family name. It's not the religions so much as the cultures surrounding them that set the two apart, the child ushered into Saint Patrick's on Sundays, drinking in the high drama of saints and stained glass. As for Edgar, his time as a driver is merely a blip in a life that will be sturdily rebuilt, making a new family and successful career in real estate after his early marriage fails. But Kittie doesn't so easily recover and is left a single mother at a time when divorce is a scandal. What can she do but leave town and take whatever job she can find, which means factory work, long hours of sewing corsets before returning to her pretty Audrey. Like the queen of heaven, such a child, enough to redeem the weight of anyone's life.

Toes first, white foot followed by a length of leg, flat stomach, fall of dark hair, Audrey steps from the dressing area. She's sixteen or seventeen—her age changes with each telling. In every version though, Audrey is simply a girl going about her business under the brim of a wide hat, unwittingly magnetizing a man by the cut of her features. He proffers his card, asking her mother's permission for her to pose. In 1907, such discovery stories might not yet be cliché, though given the Munsons' situation, it's possible that Kittie sent the girl around. But what is a goddess without a creation myth? No matter how it happened, young Audrey collided with a man and his camera; her form met his approval, which led to this moment of her stepping out of her skirts.

Do her fingers tremble as she does away with her stockings, or does the girl already demonstrate more than her fair share of pluck? Certainly Kittie must stand at her side, for Audrey's mother is never far. She might set an overworked hand onto the girl's white shoulder, saying, "You'll be fine," as Audrey pushes from behind the curtain, leaving her mother to catch her lip with a tooth, hoping the man will see what she has always seen. *Yes,* Kittie might think as the last of her daughter's body slips from view, *a girl like Audrey should rise into a better life.* And who knows, such a girl might carry her mother with her as she soars, freeing her from the corset factory job, the long hours and low pay, the tedious, backbreaking work—could a mother be blamed for pinning such hopes on a daughter's beauty, knowing its power, the way it alone persuades?

NEW YORK, 1916

Bent at the waist, she soars over the corner of Fifty-Ninth and Fifth, near the southeast corner of Central Park. Her breasts are firm as the fruit in her basket. She leans forward, showing off—how shall we say—her posterior, which faces the Plaza Hotel. Sculpted as Pomona, Goddess of Abundance, Audrey's form tops the Pulitzer Fountain and is nude except for a bit of sculpted cloth draped over one bronze leg, leaving her backside to make direct assault on the Vanderbilt's Fifth Avenue mansion, a backside said to so greatly annoy the widow of the great Corne-lius that the lady had her bedroom relocated. The very same behind that sent Mrs. Vanderbilt packing was Audrey's bread and butter.

To some, Nature bestows exceptional eyesight, a way with animals, or the ability to quickly tally a column of sums, but to Miss Munson, Fortune granted a good can, a literal moneymaker—the importance of which Audrey well understood: *"And I learned, too, of the eternal search by artists, beginning in the time of ancient Greeks, for two little dimples nest-ling in the flesh of the back, just over the hips and why, when it was seen that these two dimples were pressed by a kind of nature into my back they proved to be as valuable to me as Government bonds."* (*New York American*, 1921)

NEW YORK, 1913

Hips turned slightly to the left, right leg bent at the knee, Audrey stands before the sculptor. A rare thing, an educated young lady willing to pose nude. Artists of the past relied on women bound by desperation or obligation: mistresses, family members, or prostitutes. The Victorians placed blindfolds on their nude models so that the women would not witness the gaze of men upon their bodies. As for Audrey, poverty may have led her to modeling, but the time and place are right, and she be-comes everyone's favorite muse.

The Victorians, with their bound waists and fussy morals finally give way, and the Beaux Arts building boom in New York leads to art commissions featuring statuary of the sort perfectly suited to Audrey's classical features. Pulitzer and Hearst spin racy headlines to ensnare readers—with her hair swept into Grecian-style bands and outfitted in gossamer gowns, Audrey becomes a popular subject. She's rumored to travel only by limousine, to walk city streets with a pair of white grey-hounds, three sleek creatures pushing past fruit vendors and bellhops. Audrey becomes the toast of socialite parties.

Miss Manhattan, they call her, as she poses for the greatest sculptors of the day: Isidore Konti, Stirling Calder, Daniel Carter French, Karl Bitter, and Adolph Alexander Weinman. Not an easy job, standing for hours in drafty rooms, holding poses until the muscles ache, but Au-drey works nonstop, modeling as "Venus de Milo" for a gift to Queen

Wilhelmina of the Netherlands, as all three Graces in the Astor Lobby, as "Memory" and "Descending Night" at the Metropolitan, "Evangeline" at the Longfellow Memorial. Her figure ornaments Penn Station, the Manhattan Bridge, and municipal buildings across the country. As "Civic Fame," she's crowned with laurel and reigns from the Municipal Building in Manhattan, standing twenty-five feet tall, gilded and hovering.

She serves as the official muse of the Panama Pacific International Exposition and models for three-quarters of the fifteen hundred works of art.

When the exposition opens in 1915, the world is at war. That does not stop nearly 19 million visitors from walking through the sumptuous display, which boasts regular fireworks, cuisines from all over the world, rides on biplanes—even the Liberty Bell on loan from Philadelphia. Audrey is everywhere: on programs and murals, in the statuary ornamenting elaborate gardens, in the ring of identical "Star Maidens" topping the Court of the Universe.

LOS ANGELES, 1915

Standing on a patio, drink in one hand, Audrey shades her eyes from the Southern California sun with the other. The time in San Francisco did nothing to prepare Audrey for the heat of Los Angeles. She fastens her robe—her flesh is a commodity; it will not do to have its cream spoiled by sunlight.

The era of silent films. Lillian Gish and Mary Pickford are making names for themselves. Audrey's first film, *Inspiration*, stars her as an artists' model. Written with her in mind, the role requires her to disrobe, making *Inspiration* the first nonpornographic film to feature a nude actress, and Audrey the first nude in such a film.

While the female nude is acceptable when chiseled in stone or painted onto canvas, the breathing, living nude is considered indecent, and *Inspiration* is widely banned. Audrey stars in three films total, with *Inspiration* followed by *Purity* and *Heedless Moths*—films that make money despite the indecency charges. Still, the bad press sticks to the young woman who had so recently been the toast of the town and becomes the first in a series of downward spirals that sends the twenty-four-year-old Audrey and her mother back to New York, to rooms owned by Dr. Walter Wilkins.

Behind drawn shades, Audrey allows herself to occasionally peek toward the street and jumps up at the sound of knocking at the door. A year ago, she stood center studio. Everyone's favorite body, now all she can think of is another woman's body: Julia Wilkins, wife to Dr. Walter Wilkins, who owns the boardinghouse on West Sixty-Fifth. Upon their return from Los Angeles, Audrey and her mother rent rooms from Wilkins, who falls hard for Audrey, which leads to his wife sending both women packing. Mrs. Wilkins' body has been found, in Dr. Wilkins' backyard.

When Wilkins is arrested, investigators have questions for Audrey and Kittie, but the Munson women are nowhere to be found. Stories spin; their absence spurs suspicion and a nationwide hunt. When they're finally located, Audrey is cool. Dr. Wilkins had offered marriage. The affection was not mutual, she claims. She and her mother just happened to leave the city at the same time. Though Audrey is cleared of any official involvement in the case, she's involved enough that her hand must fly to her mouth when news of Wilkins' death reaches her.

Her former landlord and rumored lover has hung himself in his Nassau County Jail cell. Tragic, but at least the thing is over—except that tongues don't stop wagging. The doctor's suicide adds only more fuel to the fire, and the scandal that erupts over Audrey's involvement is another nail in the coffin of her reputation.

Sitting before the blank page in an upstate town, Audrey clicks the typewriter's keys while her mother spends her days working as a cook. She sits at her desk, a long finger set over her lips, searching for just the right word. Muses are meant to inspire work versus creating it themselves, but Audrey finds that she has something to say and becomes a creator, if only for a few hours. She writes a series of twenty articles for

Hearst's *New York American*, finding that readers are interested in the hazards of corsets and when it's best to drink water or just how much is required for perfect skin. Audrey's articles feature beauty tips and the inside scoop on the model's life: *All girls cannot be perfect 36s, with bodies of mystic warmth and plastic marble effect, colored with rose and a dash of flame.*

MEXICO, 1922

In a darkened room, pills in her hand. Mexico, New York. A cruel name for a place so cold. The four pills are shaped like coffins, their bottle marked with a skull and crossbones. As a liquid, mercury bichloride is used to develop photographs, but in tablet form, it's diluted and used as a general antiseptic—a foot soak or a bathroom cleanser. But Audrey's pills won't be used for cleaning. She drops them into her water and brings the glass to her mouth.

In the month of May, a month before she turns thirty-two, the last of lilacs bloom after a flush of fine weather, and the landscape is finally coming to life. A beautiful woman surrounded by lilacs—the very image of spring—but Audrey sees only winter as she brings the glass of clouded water to her mouth.

SYRACUSE, 1922

In a hospital bed, she lies as her mother flutters about the room.

Only a little more than one of four tablets which she had put in a glass of water had dissolved when swallowed, the *New York Times* reports. Her doctor credits prompt care for saving her. And while Audrey might have been a goddess when she swallowed mercury bichloride, she's a baroness when she wakes.

She begins to refer to herself as "Baroness Audrey Meri Munson-Monson," claims powerful influences are at work against her, and swears she's been swindled out of her film earnings. Her mother reports that Audrey hears voices, and it's possible her brain has been damaged by the mercury solution. But the fall from goddess to baroness is more cushioned than from goddess to mortal, so perhaps Audrey was simply allowing herself to return to earth in steps.

The willowy thirty-four-year-old leans forward; the mower keeps her from tumbling down the hill as she takes a spin on her roller skates. It's said she sells kitchen utensils door-to-door, though many doors do not open. After the suicide attempt, there are reports of Audrey and her mother heading west, teaching dance and demonstrating products in a Detroit department store and living for a time in Cincinnati. No matter her route, when Audrey finally lands, it's in a small farm town on the southeastern shore of Lake Ontario.

She may as well be a ghost, walking down Main Street in the remnants of her fine clothes, passing the church and brick storefronts wearing colors and textures as strange as the woman inside them, her elegant profile set against a backdrop of apple orchards. Is it beaded headbands or long scarves that infuriate the small town? All those eyes, the purposeful avoidance of hers, talk of the pictures she starred in. Audrey's body itself is scandalous, the way she's flaunted it about without clothes, a woman without shame—is there anything worse?

It's hard to say when the real trouble began. As a child, of course —devout or not—divorce would have shamed her. And at a time when women did not yet even have the right to vote, it's not difficult to imagine the truth of earnings withheld as retribution for refusing the advances of a powerful man as Audrey had claimed. But films and murder investigation aside, the Beaux Arts building boom was over in New York, which meant fewer commissions. A future that had been gilded only a decade before had crumbled by the time she reached her midtwenties, so that those few jobs that remained were claimed by girls stepping in with pink feet to take her place.

But all of that is behind her in Mexico, where she becomes a morality lesson in the flesh. Nothing more reassuring to a small town than the sight of someone who's tried to fly falling back to earth—and if one thing is plentiful in Mexico, New York, it's earth. Gone are the grand buildings, the bustle and boom, gone the sweet fizz of adoration. But, of course, images of Audrey remain in the city like old skins, so that she feels at times absent from her body, remembering how, just a few years before, she'd been plied with gifts and begged to attend each and every soiree; likenesses of her adorning gardens and morning rooms of the rich. Her body might be anchored by an old mower in Mexico as she straps her feet into roller skates for a downhill ride, but it also shimmers in the Hamptons, in Manhattan, and a hundred other places, so that in 1925, Audrey Munson is everywhere and nowhere at once.

MEXICO, 1930

Crouched in a field, match in hand. It's how the townspeople see her. There's no evidence Audrey started the fires, but she's easy to blame with her strange manner and the way she's always roaming the fields. What goes over as fashionable in the city makes her the woman most likely to have torched Mr. Thornhill's barn in Mexico. And who knows, maybe she did it, lit the match and launched it into a pile of dry hay. She might have skated to the end of a road, beheld a freshly painted barn, recalling suddenly the power of her lips when painted scarlet—those red-hot days, the freedoms she'd gained and lost so quickly.

How many years could one ignore dirty looks on trips to the post office to look for letters that came less often? How long could one huddle in property owned by a father who'd moved on to a new wife and children to whom Audrey would likely have been an embarrassment at best? Freshly painted barnwood might ignite such thoughts. So it's possible she lit the match and torched the barn because matches are easy to come by, but you can only skate so far in rural New York State.

HEADED NORTH, 1931

Looking out a window from the backseat, Audrey's headed to the state asylum near Ogdensburg, at Point Airy. A month after the Empire State Building is completed in New York City, the city continues to churn out iconic symbols, no matter how often or how easily humans fall around them. The Dust Bowl continues out West; the Depression lingers after the stock market crash two years earlier. Prohibition. The entire country is in a slump as Audrey heads north for court-mandated care, diagnosis unclear.

Mexico and the nearby Fruit Valley slip from view, replaced by outcroppings of layered rock and farmland of the North Country and sometimes, too, a peek of the Oswegatchie as it flows from the Adirondacks to the Saint Lawrence. Houses made of local sandstone stand like sentries along the road. A person or two, a bit of traffic, the sound of birds, but the thing about the North Country is how silent it is.

She keeps pushing north until she loses sight of Lake Ontario, passing through Watertown and Alexandria Bay, going as far as one can go without crossing into Canada.

POINT AIRY, 1940

Under a wide-brim hat, reclining on the veranda—so lush is the lawn rolling out to the Saint Lawrence, so high the ceilings of the day rooms, so open and airy the Romanesque arches—Audrey could be at an exclusive resort.

The state hospital will change with the times, letting go of its founding philosophy of fresh air, social activities, and healthful diet in favor of postwar science that prescribes drugs, shock therapy, and restraints. But when Audrey arrives, the asylum is a self-sustaining community. The residents eat from the fruit and vegetable gardens they tend, enjoy time in their own library and beauty salon, attend games of croquet, bathing parties, talks and lectures, music and church services, masquerade balls, games of bridge and pinochle, organized dances and teas. The floors are laid with oriental rugs, the rooms decorated with ferns and pianos, the grounds of Point Airy so pretty that people come by trolley from Ogdensburg to stroll the thirteen hundred acres.

Audrey lounges in a chair in high summer, hair pushed into her hat to keep her neck cool. She might forget for a time the flower gardens and expanse of lawn—because even the best sort of prison is still a prison after all. She might close her eyes and return to other summers, the gay shindigs and the long dresses, the cool drinks and warm nights, the way men from the best families begged for her presence, the pulse and promise of old New York, and her floating about, feathered and rouged. It's at such a party that she meets the man with a good name and a family mansion at Newport, a man whose role in her life varies according to sources, one she may or may not have married—the wedding was at Saint Patrick's Church, her mother claimed, while others say there was no wedding at all, that Audrey was merely his mistress. A man of means could erase a wedding or avoid it altogether. Either way,

Audrey has no husband to speak of, only a mother who does what she can and sometimes manages to get a ride north to visit her beautiful girl.

In an armchair beside the radio, she listens to reports of war in Europe. At tea in the morning room, people lean in to discuss FDR, the Lindbergh baby, Amelia Earhart's final flight. And when those same rooms are converted to cafeterias, Audrey stands in line, overhearing news of the McCarthy hearings, Eisenhower, and Nixon. In front of the television screen, she watches anchormen speak of Korea, Vietnam, and the Cold War, start to finish. Khrushchev, Brezhnev, and Gorbachev. Satellites, astronauts, and the moon landing. Martin Luther King and Kennedy, their eventual assassinations, until talk is replaced by Three Mile Island. Love Canal, the Exxon Valdez. Jimmy Carter, Ronald Reagan, Bill Clinton. She listens to music, first from radios and phonographs, later as it streams from hi-fi systems, tape decks, and cd players—songs like "Stardust" and "Goodnight, Sweetheart" giving way to Sinatra and Elvis, the Beatles and the Stones, replaced by Donna Summer and the Eagles, eventually Michael Jackson and the Spice Girls.

She's there for all of it: Iran-Contra and Monica Lewinsky. The invention of the automatic coffeemaker, the atomic bomb, personal computers. The years fall like spent leaves until she becomes so used to the view that the river must begin to feel like something of a friend as the months pass and seasons cycle, snow falling, Canadian air pushing in until the toes turn blue until finally and thankfully comes April, the earth eventually warms, the long hot days return, and time is spent reclining and remembering early days.

Except for a brief stint at a senior home a few towns over—where she's returned after crossing the busy highway to sit at the local bar —Audrey remains at the Saint Lawrence State Hospital from 1931 to 1996.

Sixty-five years. Buildings come and go. Doctors come and go. Her hair goes white; her posture sinks with the years. Nurses from the nearby school are hired, fired, and retire—some barely women when they start, girls who marry and divorce and even die as Audrey is forty, then fifty, then seventy, then ninety years old.

Here she comes again, a child in dark curls and a new dress sewn by her mother. "Look at you," people say, until the girl understands that being looked at is what she does best. What else is she ever told she's good for? Is there a hymn she likes to sing? Does she have a way with numbers? A no-fail approach to lemon torte? The ability to render landscapes with oil? The desire to study chemistry, poetry, or field botany? She tried her hand at writing and films, but no record remains of the child's talents or desires, no clue of whether she longed to occupy, at least for a time, the wide spaces beyond the body.

Sitting before a photographer, tiger cat in her lap, Audrey is twenty-four but looks younger still.

She will die a few months shy of her 105th birthday, her body will be added to her father's plot, buried beside his new wife and a half sister. Her grave will not be marked with a stone.

An army of figures bear her features, but none bears her name—not sculptures housed in museums nor statues topping fountains nor the fleet of angels hovering over rich men's graves. The buildings of Point Airy are eventually boarded up; the roof has gone soft in spots, and weeds grow into the veranda. Even the sculpture, whose marble and brass will outlast generations, will one day begin to crumble and eventually return to the earth. All but one of Audrey's films will be lost. Only a handful of photographs remain, a few nudes that look to be studies, photos in which she's posed, the look of the individual slipping away—except for the photo with the cat.

Arnold Genthe shot dozens of photos of actresses and showgirls holding his studio cat—in between sessions, perhaps for novelty or to loosen his subjects up. In another photograph by Genthe, Audrey stands cool as marble, holding a bowl as if it's an offering. In another, her gauzy robe is open, her breasts exposed in a flood of flesh and light. In these, as in other images—statues and tapestries and paintings—Audrey's body is exposed, but nothing of the woman shows through. The photograph with Genthe's tiger cat in her lap is the least posed of the bunch; she appears clothed and smiling, revealing the vulnerability of small teeth and a face that would freckle if lifted for even a second to the sun.

1915. Genthe's New York studio. In the midst of the frenzy of commissions and soirees. Between palm trees and movie cameras and claims of indecency. Before landlords and murder and flight from the city. Before pills, roller skates, and Point Airy, Audrey sits in a puddled dress, a silk rose flowering at her bodice, one hand securing a neckline that falls below the shoulder—covering a body so often disrobed. Audrey smiles into the camera. The shutter clicks open and lets in a sliver of light. There she is, minus the perfection of "Pomona," without the exotic pull of the thin-hipped "Star Maiden." She is not gilded, crowned, or winged. She is, once and for all, Audrey, caught precisely as she was for a moment in 1915, a young woman with a little tiger in her lap, entirely and miraculously herself.

What would happen if one woman

told the truth about her life?

The world would split open.

—MURIEL RUKEYSER

BIG

Even her smile is enormous, like the boy in the children's book—the first Chinese brother who swallowed the sea and held it like a lozenge inside his cheek. The woman on stage looks like she could hold the whole of Narragansett Bay in her mouth and still have room left over for singing. To say she's big is like saying the sky is wide. True, but hardly the half of it.

A little shy in the eyes before she opens her mouth, she stands before the microphone all gap-toothed warmth and coffee skin; her handkerchief is a tiny veil rocketing from white-gloved hands as she moves through a series of gospel claps. On her head: a strip of stiff lace, a sort of tiara made to match the white dress—a dress that technically fits but seems designed for a smaller body, so that the woman looks like an oversized child on her First Communion day or a tremendous bride. Either way, the woman is dressed as if she's headed to church and not the stage, though a stage can sometimes be a church, with a congregation of faces lighting the lawn. The crowd is made up of those bused in from nearby cities, musicians relaxing between sets, and the white folks, of course, young men and women from houses along the shore, the fresh-faced sons and daughters of Newport used to the grand flap of sea air.

The day is steamy, but an occasional breeze rises from the bay to cut the heat as Louis Armstrong turns the crowd to syrup with his version of "Lazy River" and Dinah Washington sings "All of Me." Mahalia sends chills down every back with her come-to-Jesus voice, while Thelonius Monk sits like a genius at his keyboard. Ray Charles and Chuck Berry take the stage. The kings and queens of American music. But such pronouncements can only be made in retrospect. On this day in 1958, the Jazz Festival in Newport is only a few years old, with no history, no reputation to live up to. The performers know only the moment, the bending into their instruments, the pluck of bass, piano, and voice. No, they're not yet legend, but the Newport kids know something's happening on stage alright, something come up from Greenville, Tuscaloosa, and New Orleans, the sound of cotton fields erupting into old New England, making the yachts in the harbor seem like nothing but origami cranes, the cut of shoreline beginning to give.

But I have not yet said her name, the woman in the white dress—the name that's least remembered, though hers is the largest voice in Rhode Island that day. Mabel. Mabel Smith. Billed as Big Maybelle. With her swagger and thump, she's not easy to categorize. Her music's not jazz so much as blues, not blues so much as soul. The Mother of Soul, she's sometimes called, America's Queen, all velvet growl and open mouth, a woman who barely needs a microphone: *Let it go. Let it go. All right y'all.*

Big Maybelle in her tiara, Big Maybelle in her church dress, Big Maybelle moves head and hands like on Sunday mornings when she was a girl, singing "Swing Low, Sweet Chariot" and "Joshua Fit the Battle of Jericho." Only the backdrop has changed. The grand Atlantic has replaced the muddy chug of the Forked Deer River as it winds its way toward the Mississippi. Now she's singing *All right y'all* in place of calling out *Sweet Lord Jesus*. But the voice is the same, the fervor the same, the spirit descending on the crowd in the cooling night air the very same.

Born between Nashville and Memphis, did the child have any choice but to sing?

Her mama called her Mabel Louise when she was born in 1924. A record man later suggested she change her name to Maybelle and add the *Big*, as if it were needed. Anyone with eyes could see that Mabel was big. Anyone with ears could hear how massive her voice. Even still, she became Big Maybelle to help sell records. And the records sold. In a series of hits, a song called "Candy" was her all-time best seller. She recorded "Whole Lotta Shakin' Goin' On" years before Jerry Lee Lewis, showing how the song was meant to be sung. But no matter how many bought her records or clapped along, Mabel was a black woman in 1958. There were places she couldn't go and people who looked right through her, except when she took the stage and opened her mouth. Then Miss Mabel Louise Smith from Jackson, Tennessee, was all anyone could see.

It's like the earth breaking open, what comes from Mabel's mouth, the sweet-sour sugar holler—so that something is fanned to life on a summer night in 1958. Something opens up, strains of recollection perhaps, old sounds given new voice. A sound so true that it's a wonder the mansions don't crumble along the Cliff Walk, nothing short of a miracle that the morning rooms and upper loggias of summer homes belonging to Astors and Vanderbilts don't heave and tumble into the sea.

All of that, and it's the crowd I watch—the field of faces lit by booze and music, an army of starched soldiers coming unstuck, something starting up in their chests. How they listen, the Newport crowd, how they watch the revelation on stage while nodding their heads, men with good teeth and ruddy skin, women in pedal pushers and pearls—mouths slightly open, a sort of radical relaxation, fingers snapping, heads rolling, slipping out of their containers a bit, the sails in the harbor fluttering in their stomachs. Still, it's 1958 New England, and even as the young people make loops of cigarette smoke and toss back drinks, their hair remains obedient, breasts remain bound by tiny bras, the women more Audrey Hepburn than Janis Joplin.

Here comes one of them now, a girl brave or far gone enough to stand on her feet when most of the crowd is sitting. With dark hair, all cheekbone and chiseled jaw, she's a sort of Jackie O. Only in 1958, Jackie's still fresh from her wedding at Saint Mary's, with the reception in one of the mansions along this very shore. In 1958, Jackie's still a Kennedy with a new baby, her husband not yet president or saint. 1958. So much still to unfold, as the real Jackie sits upshore sipping cool drinks, while the rest of the world is in flux.

Althea Gibson's won for the second straight year at Wimbledon; the first black champion, she shook the hand of the queen a year before. Ruth Taylor was hired as the first black flight attendant at Mohawk Airlines, serving on flights from Ithaca to New York (though she'll soon be let go for getting married). Satellite Records opens and publishes the sounds of the African American South. Progress, yes, though lynchings will continue for another decade, and an outbreak of riots that sweeps cities throughout the country is yet to come. Martin Luther King will be murdered in Memphis, Malcolm X in New York.

But what can any of this have to do with the young woman in a pink sweater and white pants, wiggling out of her shell, reaching for the place each of us longs for but must find on her own? The girl in the pink sweater gets closer, something inside her fanned by the voice like magma, a body spread like a table, the ripe growl and husky boom and hot damn if Mabel doesn't have something that Jackie wants, so that the girl has no choice but to swish potato-chip hips and let her lids fall like lazy curtains over her eyes while holding her hand high in the air, as if she's just hopped a bucking cloud.

It's likely that this night will not be a permanent transformation. She cuts loose and tries but might not quite get there, our Jackie, and who knows, maybe Mabel never did outside singing. But Mabel—whose dress will never fall from her body the way Jackie's sweater drapes her elegant frame, who cannot order from the same menu or rest her head in the same beds as such girls, who will one day slip into a diabetic coma and die of sugar before she's fifty—right now, Mabel Louise Smith from Jackson, Tennessee, is up on stage, sound pounding from each of her gilded cells, the ocean and sky conspiring behind her, the world not so much splitting open as starting to develop a series of promising cracks.

One woman, usually invisible, standing before the crowd.

One woman, making full use of her voice, enough to render mansions and yachts and perfectly coiffed hair beside the point. Mabel is easily three hundred pounds, and still her body is no match for the voice, which should come as no surprise because when a voice is used—really used—how could it be otherwise?

In the fall of 1934, a letter originated on a ship bound for Italy.

Busy with travel, the writer apologized for sending a group letter, a copy of which was found folded inside a book eighty years later. Nothing is known of the woman who posted the letter from Bologna on New Year's Day, 1935, except her name and the thoughts in its pages.

MANUELA, WITH A HIP

1. The letter is stolen in the most basic sense. Mailed from Bologna in 1935, written by someone named Manuela Gray. A person I want to know, almost know, but cannot know apart from the fourteen mimeographed sheets that have shuffled through time and landed in my hand.

Which is not to say I cannot see her. An image of her rises before me, distilled from the collection of sentences and what I know of her era, so that she becomes Claudette Colbert in *It Happened One Night*, suit jacket gathered at the waist, open neckline, and bobbed hair. 1934. The floppy garb of flappers has given way to fitted jackets and smart skirts, so that Manuela is an assemblage of angles and curves as she purses painted lips and reclines on a deck chair in leather pumps, a girl with a letter in her hand. Only she's more woman than girl, and the letter may not yet be in her hand. So little is certain, except that the raw ingredients for a letter are stewing in Manuela's head. Surrounded by an expanse of sea no less blue for days spent looking into it, the sight of Roman ruins, the clean sea air, the endless sky overhead—our writer is filled with all that swells the heart or head or whichever part gives birth to such things as letters. Breezes circle the promenade, mussing ladies' hair, making off with hats and the feathers pinned to them so that Manuela must pull her wool wrap closer as she sits on the ship's deck watching the last bit of Sicily slip into the distance.

———

2. "From Margaret Hill," my mother-in-law says as she hands me the letter. "A lady who used to live in the village."

My mother-in-law is the most purposeful and generous of people. When someone falls sick or is alone, she considers the person, his or her manners, and tastes, then plucks a book from her shelf and brings it to the person, reads aloud gentle mysteries by Agatha Christie or Tony Hillerman after serving up ginger cookies and news of the world. Margaret Hill was one of her beneficiaries; my mother-in-law stopped by to read to her whenever she could. A copy of Manuela's letter was found folded into a book inside a box given to my mother-in-law when Mrs. Hill passed.

I resist the letter at first, thanking my mother-in-law and meaning it but failing to read the letter right away because it's long and I have a pile of other things to read—and the truth is that I'm often disappointed by what comes heartily recommended, movies and jokes and books. But finally, a certain openness arises that coincides with the letter left on the table, and I fall into its pages. I read all the way through, then go back to the first page and start again. My husband and I read the letter together, captivated by Manuela's descriptions and wit. Even her name charms. *Manuela Gray.* Like the title of an old film, or a lost Brontë sister. We begin to speak of her as a friend, *our Manuela*, and read passages aloud, making this woman we do not know part of our life. *What would Manuela make of this poem in the* New Yorker? *What would Manuela think of reality TV? What word would she use to describe the color of bluebirds in the park, caught for a second in the sun?*

3. The *SS Saturnia* will soon be retooled for military use by Mussolini, but in the autumn of 1934, the ship still brims with international passengers on the Italian line. The sun shines as they move toward Trieste; the ship passes in and out of jagged coastline, offering up views of whitewashed buildings, old stone walls, and water so blue it hurts to look.

Manuela arrives just in time, boarding the *Saturnia* while such things as cocked hats and deck chairs remain. It is here, perhaps, as they pass through the harbor of Korčula, looking from red-tile roofs into the sea, that she finds some paper and begins the letter she's been composing in her head for weeks: *Dearest Kitty, Grace, Gene, Aline . . .*

1934. Dolfuss has been assassinated in Austria. Mussolini tightens his chokehold on Italy. Hitler declares himself Führer in Germany. The Great Depression lingers back home. John Dillinger breaks out of jail using a wooden pistol. Millions of acres of farmland are swallowed by a two-day dust storm in Oklahoma and Texas. *Anything Goes* opens in New York. All of this is background as Manuela boards an ocean liner and moves forward, steady as the *Saturnia*, unwavering as time itself:

When I look at the calendar I know that it is nearly two months since I sailed away. It tells me this. I cannot measure time at all. I feel divorced from my old self.

4. The Adriatic shivers as the ship breaks its surface. Pages of the letter write themselves as the days pass:

At Naples, I was entertained by the Signorini family who had a splendid view of Mt. Vesuvius. Manuela visits a mosque in Algiers, buys *a cake of soap in the oldest pharmacy in Europe*, attends cocktail parties with the Italian consul, and his wife, and *the Vice-Consul, many stunning French officers, and the dear old Capt. of the* Saturnia. *We had no fear about becoming too merry in our cups as [the ship] could not go without our Captain.*

Consuls and captains and cocktail parties—she is both ordinary and extraordinary, this woman traveling alone in 1934, traipsing about the caves of Postumia:

One is a natural ballroom, lighted by a huge crystal chandelier . . . all sorts of weird shapes—a perfect hunchbacked man which we touched for luck.

Who is this "we" she speaks of? Does the limestone shine from the rub of so many fingers? What does she think as her hand comes upon the cool hunched back?

Such moments are gone; the answers to questions eight decades removed must be left to the imagination. Even the letter itself is a shadow of light already spent, the words composed in past tense, so much has already been claimed by memory by the time Manuela finally sits before a typewriter:

I adored Palermo, it was spring there.

———

5. She travels by car *by the sea at first, then inland and finally over the new Mussolini Bridge* and on to Venice.

I had a room on the Grand Canal and spent hours lying there and looking out. But she leaves her room, taking time to soak in the city:

I heard Mass at St. Mark's, fed the pigeons, had tea at Florian's, stood on the Bridge of Sighs, walked over the Rialto, muttering the Merchant of Venice *to myself.*

It's in Venice that she's clearest to me, tilting her head for a better look at Titian's *Assumption*, eyes fixed on the quiver of scarlet robe as the Virgin rises into the sky. There she is on the Rialto, leaning against stone archways amid the slap of water and the unrelenting moonlight, a woman on a bridge reciting Shakespeare: *Tell me where is fancy bred / Or in the heart or in the head?*

6. But all cannot be moonlight. Despite the travel clothes, parties with dignitaries, and the recitation of Shakespeare on the Rialto—despite all this, Manuela's destination is a hospital, the Instituto Ortopedico Rizzoli in Bologna. She suffers from arthritis, it seems, something to do with a hip. In her letter, she thanks *Grace, my most amiable, calm saint, you remembered so well my fondness for poetry and Edna St. Vincent Millay. And the funny card of different hips and diets which was here to greet me when I arrived so lonely and plain skeered.*

So, she is afflicted. And afraid sometimes, this woman bold enough to travel so far from home, this Catholic who makes reports of receiving Communion but who also carries the photograph of a man she once loved and allows herself the sizzle of sonnets by Millay—*What lips my lips have kissed, and where, and why.*

7. I've made her into a sort of icon, Our Lady of the *Saturnia*, twin to Claudette Colbert, woman of the smart suit, wearer of the side-cocked hat, patron of solo travelers, poetry lovers, and women facing the unknown. But what can truly be revealed by rubbing scraps of paper together? What do I actually know, except that her hip is problem enough to lead her far from home and that someday, perhaps in Bologna, her skirts will begin to loosen with the loss of flesh, the heels of her shoes lowering until she wears only her own padded soles, a sinking of the body, until all that remains can be contained in one hand, the whisper of paper and eighty-year old ink.

Days aboard the *Saturnia* spend themselves, as all days do. Now, a hospital: *The Instituto was built in 1000 or 1100 and was a Benedictine monastery until Napoleon drove the monks away.* Despite the cloistered walk beneath her room where Benedictines once strolled and prayed, despite the marble *flung with a lavish hand*, frescoes by Carracci and Reni, and the scent, in certain corners, of old books, San Michele al Bosco is a hospital, one that must become for Manuela a home.

8. Armed with Millay, her writing case, and the photograph she carries, she's led to her room. I see her moving toward the door, entering the room with tact and grace, admiring out loud the light falling from the window. But if I look more closely as she stands in the doorway, I might notice a small sigh escape her lips as the glitter of all those ports of call take their place in the past and all that's left before her is a hospital room. And I wonder if she considers, if only for a second, the possibility of falling to the floor. Does she feel the unexpected weight of light streaming through the window, setting fire to the dust motes? I see her staring into the constellation of illuminated specks and speaking a few lines of poetry to herself as she did on the canal in Venice, this time a few lines of Millay: *but the rain / is full of ghosts tonight that tap and sigh / upon the glass and listen for reply.*

Manuela's letter reveals no evidence that her mobility is impaired, but why else the trip to Bologna, the postcard of hips, and the hospital stay? She'll later mention the risks involved with treatment, and there is, in every word not written, a sense of finality to this trip. Had she hobbled, then, along the Bridge of Sighs? I can't see it. Manuela steps lively in her writing, and despite whatever burden has brought her to Bologna, there's only one mention of isolation, though it is spoken of as a regular companion:

The loneliness comes early in the morning when I first awake and realize that another day is ahead of me and in the evening at nine when the Institute settles down for the night.

———

9. Under its renowned director, Vittorio Putti, the Institute at San Michel del Bosco has made Bologna a mecca for orthopedic care—though no other Americans or even English-speaking patients are mentioned. Only those of a certain means, or the most desperate, or some combination of both could afford such a long trip, which tells us something about Manuela, who speaks of Professor Putti as *one of the handsomest older men I have ever seen.* A pioneer in the field of orthopedics, he'll die a few years after Manuela's letter is postmarked, but the man is fully alive as she writes: *his hair is snow white and plentiful; his eyes brown coals of fire . . . kind to me in so many little ways . . . he arranged to have the Contessa Carolina Rasponi call on me the very first day.*

Among the patients are politicians, men of the cloth, and Italian nobility: *Georgia's summer villa at Riccioni is opposite Mussolini's. She sees him frequently swimming in the Adriatic. He wears a green bathing suit not black. She adores children and plays often with the little Mussolinis and with the children of Dolfuss who, you may recall, were at this resort . . . when the tragedy occurred.*

Manuela's companions could fill a novel: *The Duchessa Madrigliari broke her back years ago hunting in England. . . . She has skin like gardenia, unrouged, but lips rounded perfectly. Her hair is raven black with flashes of silver. . . . Her eyes are very dark and very soft (especially when she smiles at Professor Putti), her teeth the pearls one reads about in Mary J. Holmes.*

10. A war is brewing, one whose scale is impossible to fathom. But in Bologna, the days pass with Manuela receiving guests and composing a letter to her friends:

One of my consolations is Don Camillo, a young Benedictine monk, a human saint, who sings and plays like an angel. . . . I write my Confession in Italian; read it to him; he finally burns it. He visits all the sick and comes to me last of all so that he will not be too late for all the others. This is usually at dinner time and he serves and waits on me, even peeling the fruit.

It's tempting to wonder over the content of Manuela's confessions, the secrets and sins she harbored and wrote out in Italian—but there's no time because there's the image of her confessor peeling her fruit. He sits bedside, almond-eyed as a Byzantine icon, removing the skin of a clementine, splitting the fruit with his hands, and serving her wedges from his fingers. In Manuela's telling, all Bologna is filled with beautiful saints: *Once in a while Professor Putti calls for me at night and I put a big coat over my camicia and spend a pleasant hour in his private apartments, listening to the fine music from Florence and Rome. Don Camillo is usually in the corner stroking Millis, the police dog. Sometimes the younger doctors come in and we play an Italian gambling game. Last night we played for chestnuts. There was never a more delicious combination than hot roasted chestnuts and red wine.*

11. Despite the pull of red wine and roasted chestnuts, of fruit-bearing monks and talk of seaside resorts, Manuela inhabits a hospital and not an old film: *Little Rosetta has never sat up in 2 years and she is only 2½ years old. Heavy sand bags lie on her legs all day to keep them in a certain position. It is heartbreaking to see her attempt to rise when something attracts her attention. . . . Nina Francoso, 22 years old, had her leg amputated because of a malignant tumor-sarcoma. She was engaged to be married, too. She called me in so cheerfully to see "mia gamba" her new wooden leg. . . . A man of 32 has been here in bed for over 2 years—every joint in his body stiffened with arthritis. He has to be fed. . . . He finds it difficult to chew and fears that soon he will unable to swallow solid food. Yet his bed was pulled into the chapel on Christmas Eve and he sang the Italian Christmas Hymns with all the others at Mid-night Mass.*

Manuela does not mind sentimentality as she describes the Christmas scene, compares ladies' skin to gardenias, and indulges in little sermons: *You who are straight and strong should be so thankful. Happiness is a hot bath in the tub whenever you want it; a brisk walk in the out of doors; a shampoo for your hair when necessary; your meals at a table with other humans; a big glass of Am. Orange juice in the morning; hot coffee; no crumbs in bed; a good night's sleep; liberty to read until morning if you desire; etc.*

12. But every letter requires a reader to complete it. That's the agreement. The letter begins with the writer, of course, but more than mere witness, the reader becomes the letter's pulse point, recipient of image and thought and its particular arrangement of symbols. A letter starts with its maker, but the reader is the continuation of its breath:

Today is New Year's Day, January 1, 1935, and as I write this date for the first time I pray that it brings health, happiness and prosperity to us all.

New Year's Day.

Manuela is on the edge of something as she completes her letter on the first morning of 1935. Radiant, such days. Dazzling, the possibilities. Something has changed for our writer, something she's been working toward and on this day allows herself to reveal:

Now the miracle—I am much better than I have been in several years since I have had this long rest in bed. For ten days I have had practically no pain. Prof. Putti is dubious but astounded.

A miracle, she says, but what she allows is hope. In all of her letter, she is gracious but does not allow herself such possibilities, except in its very last lines. We cannot know if Manuela's pain will disappear for good, or whether she will report its return in the next letter home. We cannot know whether she books return passage to New York, if she makes a further tour of Europe, or if the room overlooking a centuries-old cloister will be her last.

❡ 3. We must leave her here, New Year's Day, 1935.

Before Mussolini invades Ethiopia. Before the Blitzkrieg and Pearl Harbor. Before Auschwitz and Hiroshima. The letter that has been writing itself for months is postmarked on a day when it's equally possible that Manuela encountered miracles or another series of disappointments. A terrible thing for the curious, such mystery, but a reminder to savor what one is given, roasted chestnuts, the scent of citrus as a monk with the beautiful voice peels away the rind, Don Camillo and Professor Putti, Millay and Shakespeare, and the writer herself, perched forever on the edge of 1935, treading the moments before innocence is lost, doors flung open as she contemplates the coming year and all it might bring:

Last night we had a party in my room and saw the Old Year die and the New Year born with Orvieto wine and panetone. My friends were a doctor with a knee the result of a motor cycle accident; an engineer with a back the result of skeeing; a man with a back and an arm as a result of being thrown from his horse; and

  Manuela
  with a hip who loves you all so much.

And the blue pansy mouth sang to the sea:

Mother of God, I'm so little a thing,

Let me sing longer,

Only a little longer.

—CARL SANDBURG, FROM "ADELAIDE CRAPSEY"

ON SEEING
WEATHER-BEATEN TREES
A STUDY IN
TWO PHOTOGRAPHS

I.

A photograph from your Vassar days. 1900, or so. A lively girl. Funny, they say. Editor of the yearbook, basketball captain, actor in school plays, member of the debating club, class poet for three years straight. What a figure you cut, Adelaide—the piled hair, cinched waist, and flounced skirt. One imagines such girls to go on forever, with the long white dress, the frop upon the head; the photograph must be from your title role in the play *Kitty Clive*. You write poems and wear white dresses, but you are no retiring angel. Your thesis at Vassar combines history, writing, and socialism.

What things must come out of your mouth, Adelaide. What shocking and beautiful things. But then, of course, back home, your mother aids orphans, while your father champions Darwin and Marx from the pulpit, his views so liberal they will one day spell trouble. But that is years away. Only after the photograph do the troubles begin. Only after you're gone will Sandburg write of you—though he got it wrong: you are no trembling flower. But all of that is to come. First, there are archeological studies in Rome, a teaching job at Smith, your analysis of poetic meter in Europe. First, you must charm London. First, you must notice the horse-chestnut trees in the Champs-Élysées and scribble out poems in the fading Parisian light:

Is it as plainly in our living shown,
By slant and twist, which way the wind hath blown?

II.

Only fourteen years have passed since Vassar, but already your face has thinned, the fullness replaced by a sinking of sorts. The smile remains, with your teeth peeking out. The look on your face: shyness in front of the camera. Exposed. Caught up in the grainy strain of its enlargement, all shadow and inky striation. 1914. Many have died, your sister, Emily, and your oldest brother. Your father has been marked a radical, suffered a heresy trial, and stripped of his pulpit. So little left to lose. Except the poems, which come in the face of fever, so that those you write at Saranac Lake bear burdens that belie them. Gauzy and spare, more like haiku than the Victorian verse of your Vassar days.

Ah, but there you are, coughing into a cloth. There you are, sitting outside, allowing the cold to seep into your chest. Decades before medicine will wipe away the need for cure cottages, porches are the preferred treatment for tuberculosis; patients lie for hours in fresh air, regardless of the chill of their bones or the season. So it's on the porch we find you, in your mantle of black, already more ghost than woman, writing poems in the form you invent. The American cinquain, and you are its mother. Twenty-two syllables are all you can afford for the fever that will claim you this fall is having its way. But not yet. Look at you, Adelaide, taking up the pen when you can barely stand. Look at you, teasing death into five lines, working it into a string of black beads—even as it consumes you—you know what strength is and hold it and bend it to your will with the work of your hands:

I know
Not these my hands
And yet I think there was
A woman like me once had hands
Like these.

In the 1840s South, cotton was king. The mechanical gin drove the output exponentially, leading to a surge in demand for slave labor—the machine separated the fiber from the seeds, but hands were still needed for all the planting and picking. With the Atlantic slave trade ended, plantations looked to the domestic slave trade. Hundreds of thousands of people were sold from the Upper South to Mississippi, Texas, and Arkansas—any of the great swaths of warm land required for growing cotton. Families were once again broken apart and loaded onto ships bound for Mobile and New Orleans before they could even say good-bye.

HEROINES OF THE ANCIENT WORLD

I.

At first, the girl might think a sort of confetti has made its way into the school and landed on her bedclothes, bits of colored paper or petals shaken from roses. But even a hopeful girl can avoid reality for only so long, and as she looks into her handkerchief, May begins to understand that the spray of red has come from her own body. She tries to remember what she's heard about blood in the cough, what people have said, whether it indicates possibility or certain death. The memory of Celestia arrives unbidden—her teacher who'd died from consumption two years before. Miss Bloss had coughed scarlet too, and it may be the tug of questions and the weariness that arises from them—more than any tea or potion—that finally helps the girl sleep.

I find her at Mount Hope, 157 years later, buried in the same stretch of cemetery as Susan B. Anthony, a stone's throw from Frederick Douglass, the earth rich with the deposit of ancient glaciers. Nothing about the grave grabs my attention—no mossy turn of Celtic cross, no black silk crow perched on an angel's shoulder—May's stone is plain, nothing but the words themselves to stop me cold:

> The white slave girl
> known as
> MAY FIELDING
> Died June 2, 1857
> Aged 15

White slave.

What does that mean? Irish? No. The word "slave" would probably not be used for servants.

White slave.

How white? White, as in a beautiful tooth or as newly tatted lace? Victorian white, as in women who rubbed arsenic into their skin to make it the color of snow? How to make sense of a slave in 1857 New York State? Or a child, dead at fifteen?

II.

I walk at Mount Hope for ferns and Solomon's seal in spring, for the cover of trees in high summer, the flame of maples in October, and—if you are not troubled by such settings, and seek, as I do, the stark shadows of winter—there's no better place to contemplate old marble, the inevitability of collapse, frost heaving the stones, the unrelenting colonies of lichen. A place to consider one called Susan V. buried so close to the nation's most famous suffragist—poor old Susan V., only fifty steps and one initial removed from the other Susan, yet no one stops to linger or leave handfuls of violets. The random patterns of admiration. Such are my thoughts as I walk, listening to the talk of old stone until a few begin to seem like friends.

Once I found May's stone though, the press of questions interrupted my walk until she became the point of the walk, my thoughts returning to the mystery of the girl who died in 1857. I wondered and asked questions and looked her up, again and again, until I found an article in the cemetery newsletter written by a history student from the nearby university that revealed something of the girl's identity: May was the fair-skinned daughter of a mulatto slave in service at a Washington, D.C., hotel, and a member of the Twenty-Seventh United States Congress.

III.

It's the cough that consumes you, the constant work of chest and throat, handkerchief flying to the mouth, the ribcage racked from exertion. Heat settles onto the skin—but only the skin—the body itself never fully warming, tossing and turning and soaking the bedclothes with sweat. The faces of visitors float like balloons overhead, pity etched into their faces, the features prematurely pinched and grieving, as if the one in bed is already dead. Various cures are tried, as are kind words and good intentions, while food sits like so many stones on a tray. The book lent by a friend may as well be brick, for how impossible it is to lift. And the prayers (always prayers) as the afflicted slips in and out of the undertow of dreams, a series of drownings and coming-tos.

IV.

Her skin, not that of a brunette but that of a blonde, claimed sisterhood with the fairest of our Saxon daughters, claimed the *Journal of the Rochester Home for the Friendless* in an 1858 article about May, which supplies most of what's known about the girl who stayed at the charity home for the month before her death.

May's skin is light enough to pass.

May's skin might be white, but no matter its shade; if her mother were known, she'd be considered a quadroon, the one-quarter black child of a mulatto slave, and a slave herself.

In popular imagination and literature, quadroon girls are portrayed as dark-haired beauties scented with spice, surrounded by jasmine and Spanish moss. Abolitionists pointed to the cases of such children to demonstrate the horrors of slavery, conjuring images of girls waiting under orange blossoms to be exchanged for gold by their fathers, sold off as "fancy maids," or slaves used for sex:

> *Her eyes were large, and full of light,*
> *Her arms and neck were bare;*
> *No garment she wore save a kirtle bright,*
> *And her own long, raven hair.*

V.

Clover Street School, 1854.

I imagine May walking with friends, arms linked—the winter was a long one; the girls are eager for fine weather and stop to step over wide puddles as they stroll the grounds. A robin lands on the lawn or an early blue bird as they discuss what their headmistress has most recently taught them or gather in to tell a secret.

"What?" May asks, giggling over the words repeated.

A cluster of girls under a budding maple, lace collars held in place with a brooch. How clear they seem to me, May standing among them in a dress with a fitted waist and layers of crinoline, petticoats puffing out her skirt. She smooths her bodice with the flat of a hand, remembering the ease of the shorter dresses and pantalets she'd only recently outgrown. Someone says something silly, and the group laughs and moves on, the young ladies of Clover Street in their flounces and ruffles, looking bright as springtime itself.

VI.

The Lion of the West, Rochester becomes America's first boomtown, thanks to the Erie Canal, which greatly reduces the time and cost of travel and movement of goods from New York, fueling the first great westward migration. The population soars, and Rochester becomes home to the likes of Frederick Douglass and Susan B. Anthony. Abolition is strong in the region, with a network of stations along the Underground Railroad allowing fugitive slaves to move from house to house on their way over the lake and into Canada. But no matter how progressive its various outcrops, public education does not yet extend beyond eighth grade. Only the wealthiest families can send their children to private schools for further education, and even then, it's usually reserved for boys. When a girl's education is extended, it's most often to master the feminine behavior expected of her class, making her into a suitable wife. But things are different at Celestia Bloss's school, which educates its girls at least as well as the boys. As a result, its reputation grows, and the Clover Street Seminary becomes one of the finest schools in the region, attracting students from hundreds of miles and states away, as well as local students who travel by horse-drawn buses or packet boats along the canal.

VII.

May is the girl caught up in the sight of clouds and dawdling at the very back. Or else she's the one out front with a generous stride, leading the pack. Perhaps she is the serious sort, thinking over what was said in astronomy class, running through the piano scales, practicing her elocution. Her dark curls are parted down the middle, pinned at the back of her head, and covered with a bonnet as the line of students shuffles back toward the stately Greek Revival, which stands on a lot rich with trees, with a branch of Allyn's Creek running through its acres.

May, like the other homesick girls, might wear something from her mother or grandmother—a ribbon around the neck or an old ring, perhaps a stickpin from a teacher, a castoff or present given because, despite appearances, May does not have what the other girls do. Celestia Bloss knows this. The director of the Clover Street School, Miss Bloss is married to Mr. Brewster, but no one at the school calls her Mrs. Brewster. But then, Celestia Bloss is not like other ladies.

VIII.

A well-known abolitionist, William Clough Bloss sheltered fugitive slaves in his home and fought to have New York State admit black children into regular district schools with whites. A friend to Frederick Douglass, Bloss published an early abolitionist newspaper in 1834. Susan B. Anthony also knew William Bloss, who'd advocated for women's suffrage when she was still a child. The family later arranged and financed the radical suffragist Emmeline Pankhurst's visit to the city. Celestia's use of her maiden name was itself a radical decision—one made at least a decade before Lucy Stone famously kept her own last name upon marriage in 1855.

Celestia Bloss was not only teacher and headmistress at Clover Street Seminary; she also researched, wrote, and published at a time when most women were spoken of and for by others and lacked the right to own property, keep their earnings, or vote. *Bloss' Ancient World*, published in 1845, was followed by *Heroines of the Crusades* in 1852. Both were attributed to C. A. Bloss, with the later book dedicated to her students, including May. In fact, Celestia researched and wrote the lives of Eleanor of Aquitaine and Adela of Blois while May lived and studied at the Clover Street School.

What classes they must have been—even as she sent her manuscripts off under the cover of a pseudonym, Celestia would have been on fire with knowledge. May and the other students were her most regular audience, listening as she described the lives of saints and queens, brave and spirited girls and women who had somehow made their lives their own.

IX.

But she could not save herself. Celestia's body collapsed into itself, growing thinner than her pupils, becoming all large eyes and pale skin before she died—a fiercely intelligent woman who understood better than most about hope and perseverance yet succumbed at the age of forty-three.

I can nearly see May again. This time standing in a shadowed alcove, looking on as people file into the foyer in their darkest clothes. She watches as they line up to say good-bye to her friend and wonders what might come next. (Was there a plan hatched in those final days, the possibility of teaching, a certain talent the girl showed, the hope of her eventually marrying?)

It's not known whether Celestia actually knew May's true identity. It's possible that she knew May's secret and relished the ability to educate a girl whose fair skin made it so that she did not have to hide under false floors while inching her way over the water. But even if she didn't know May's heritage, Celestia understood the child had no one else, and whether she saw the girl as black or white, she would have been the one person most likely to embolden than hamper her dreams so that May would have been doubly stricken at her loss.

X.

Celestia's death is not the first such loss for May. At thirteen years old, she's used to saying good-bye, coming even to expect such endings. Such hard realities might help her cope when, two years later, she wakes to the weight of her own body grown heavy, with a fit of coughing and a chill opening like an icy flower in her chest.

When May does not improve and with no one to claim her, the Rochester Home for the Friendless takes her in. A buggy conveys her from Clover Street to the corner of East Avenue and Alexander Street near the center of city, a trip that might otherwise have been exciting but cannot matter much to May, given that she's in the last days of consumption and spends most of her time shivering in bed.

XI

The Home for the Friendless had as its mission the taking in and care of "virtuous and unprotected" women and girls who happened on hard times. Social class was not a factor in admission, and it's unclear if race was a factor—likely it was—though the patrons of Rochester who'd started the benevolent society had decided that immigrants would be admitted. In any case, a girl like May, straight from one of the finest schools in the region, a fair girl coughing into a handkerchief, the very image of Victorian frailty, would have been welcome at the home, where she's listed in the records as *May Fielding*. Occasionally recorded as *Mary* due to clerical error, the mistake was remedied with slash marks through the mistaken 'r's. *Fielding* was later revealed as an alias to protect the girl, though from which danger is not clear—the potential scandal for her politician father or bounty hunters in search of runaway slaves? May's departure from Washington coincides with the passage of the new Fugitive Slave Act, and there's the fact that she was taken to the progressive city of the West.

XII

May traveled north with a Mrs. Pratt—first to New York City, then west to Celestia Bloss's school on a landing just south of Irondequoit Bay. Besides reconciling faces and cities completely new to her, the child would have been surprised at how cold it was and by the snow that fell gently at first, soft and fluttering in November, only to harden after the holidays, freezing the cobblestones and even the canal until the whole of the city became an icy clamp.

How May ended up in the care of Mrs. Pratt and Celestia remains a mystery, and there's no record of Mrs. Pratt again until May's death, at which time the Home for the Friendless sent a bill for May's care—the home charged those who could pay a dollar per week for adults, fifty cents for children. The Clover Street School paid its portion of May's two-dollar fee with a donation of vegetables, while Mrs. Pratt failed to respond at all until the year after May's death.

XIII.

In 1858, Mrs. Pratt wrote the Home for the Friendless, enclosing ten dollars to cover May's fees and funeral expenses. The note that accompanied the payment shared what she knew of May's origins—*the daughter of a mulatto woman in service at a Washington hotel*, she wrote, *and an American member of Congress.* Just a few lines, but May's story began to take shape.

In 1842, when the United States flag had only twenty-six stars, a girl was born to an enslaved woman and a member of the Twenty-Seventh United States Congress. In an act of protection, the woman claimed that the baby had died and sneaked her off to her grandmother for care. Whether this was done to spare the child or the man is unclear. Mrs. Pratt's letter reveals only that May was removed from Washington to keep her safe and to avoid "scandal," which implies that her father's name might have somehow been connected to her mother. But which grandmother? The black one seems likely, though it's unknown whether she was free or, if enslaved, how the sudden appearance of a white child would have been explained. Is it possible that her white grandmother took May in? The mother of the congressman who'd lain with a slave at a Washington hotel?

The truth is probably this: An important man stays in a hotel, and after a rich dinner heads off for a good night's sleep, making use of whatever he wants before getting there. May's mother may not mind the attention from such a high-flying man or knows how useless it is to resist. A mixed-race woman, she herself is the product of such a liaison. Or their relations may be long-standing. She might feel something like love for the congressman, and he for her. But all of this is guesswork, making lace of faded threads. What's most certain is that the child is hidden away the day she's born, her family on both sides deciding the girl is a secret too dangerous to claim.

XVI.

Once upon a time there was a girl who was taken from her mother to keep her safe, who lived with a grandmother, then with strangers so far north that the girl must have thought she'd landed in Canada. She was taken to the school on Clover Street, where she met Celestia, a woman later recorded as her "only friend"—but even then, when Celestia was gone, May had no choice but to push forward. She continued her studies, staying on at the school until she herself became sick and moved to the benevolent society home, where, by all accounts she was a model patient and duly loved, as evidenced by her stone, one of the few in the charity plot. A stone that calls her slave, calls her white, but says nothing of what lived inside a girl who was born at a time when the nation was still dividing itself into regions, drawing lines between port city and frontier town, old and new, North and South, free state and slave.

xv.

Only the name pays homage: May. Whether it was hers for all fifteen years of her life or just five, she was named for the fairest month. A name for honeysuckle and possibility. A girl constructed of the harshest realities and educated in a manner reserved for the most fortunate few. Burdened and privileged. Black and white. Slave and free. A lovely girl—though no photograph remains, it's obvious how lovely. A group of girls link arms and stroll the Clover Street grounds, giggling while practicing their Latin conjugations (*amō, amās, amat*), repeating to themselves what Miss Bloss has said about intelligence and bravery and all that women have done and what they one day will do. May. A girl in a dress shouting to her friends that the barge has just now arrived and joining the group as they run to look for a letter, perhaps, or some stray news of home.

A girl with a story, young May. A person who once walked these same streets as me. A girl pushing forward. A leaf about to unfold. In another time and place, what such a girl might have done, what she may have become.

What to call those we almost know? Those who pass in cars, in the grocery store, or on the street, looking at us full on for a moment before moving on—a spark of recognition and the slow fade. What's the word for those circling the periphery, figures who somehow stay with us, shadowing our orbits, strangers almost in reach?

TWYLA

Now that I no longer live there, I wonder if the calls still come. The ringing in the middle of the night, just as the deepest part of my body settled into sleep—thank God I kept the phone close to my bed, thank God I had only to reach out to pull it from its cradle—the way it rang between waking hours, that telephone. Not so often that a pattern could be established but enough that I began to recognize the voice when it came, the way he said, "Twyla there?" without allowing a speck of breath between the words: *Twylathere?* The voice, as if hammered from bronze, only warmer, the month of August, all patina and heat, as if the night itself had reached out and dialed my number. *Twylathere?* The calls came sandwiched between dreams, so that, even as I lifted the receiver and said, *Sorry* and *Wrong number* I wondered whether all of it—the ringing telephone, the man's voice, even Twyla herself—was not part of a dream.

Years later and a thousand miles away, I fall asleep more easily for the satisfaction of crape myrtles, the churning of coal trains, the click of insects just outside the window. But what is ever really gone forever? There are those nights when I lie awake thinking of snow, what a fine blanket it makes, the way one can learn to count on the company of cattails, the solidity of sugar maples. And while I know I can't go back, not really, not fully, there are those nights when I lie in bed wondering what would have happened if, just once, I'd pulled my body awake and unfolded myself to the darkness, saying, "Yes—this is Twyla, this is she."

A kind of light spread out from her. And everything changed color.

And the world opened out. And a day was good to awaken to.

And there were no limits to anything. And the people of the world

were good and handsome. And I was not afraid any more.

—JOHN STEINBECK

THE OPPOSITE OF FEAR

And when she appears finally before them, it's not only her confidence that heightens their blood but the skirt barely covering her rounded thighs. In her flesh-colored stockings, the young woman's legs look magnificently undressed as she steps onto the rope strung over the Niagara River Gorge. What might happen to such a pretty costume in the wind? The hair tucked under her hat might come undone—black spilling into the air, skirt flapping red over the rush of river.

They might have come to squelch the heat with a spray of Niagara's mist or because they could not travel all the way to Philadelphia for the Centennial Exposition. Or else they came, craning their necks, because nothing is so thrilling to a crowd as a possible fall.

La Spelterina! They shout.

Maria! They call, forgetting for a moment the reasons they've parted with their dollars to stand for hours in the heat, *La bella Maria!*

The crowd rests its collective eye on the figure straddling the sky like a vibrant bird. A thousand voices climb upward, ten thousand *Hurrahs* and *Good Gods* as the Niagara River slams into the gorge and Maria steps along the tightrope. The noise of the crowd joins the clang of brass bands and the call of vendors selling their wares, a great racket ascending both sides of the Niagara as Maria follows the muscled rope, pushing one foot forward, then the next.

July 1876. One of the hottest summers on record, so hot the horses are too lazy to swish at flies with their tails. A braid of scent rises in the air: the musk of so many bodies pressed together, the salt of roasted nuts, and the river itself, a green smell, all chlorophyll and rushing water.

Another step forward and the pole she carries dips at one end—the whole of her body sways with the line as a gust of wind comes up from the gorge, but she rights herself as easy as breath, paying no mind to the mad water below.

Who is she, this girl?

And what does she carry for luck as she pivots her ankle 160 feet over Niagara Falls? A wren's feather to ward off drowning? A few strands of her sister's hair braided into her bodice, a love note folded under one of her feet? Perhaps she walks, like a bride down the church aisle, with a penny tucked into a shoe. Or maybe memory is her only charm—the image of her father, pants cuffed over square calves as they practice tumbling on the pitted sand near the sea at Livorno. It's possible she says Hail Marys as she moves, the chant of prayer blocking out the sound of the river thundering in her ears. Maybe our daredevil is a practical sort and carries no amulet apart from the courage she fingers like beads as she treads the space between river and sky without a net.

The body clenches when it feels fear, the whole of it becoming as if a fist. The heart quickens, pumping faster and diverting blood to the muscles. Breath grows rapid; the stomach empties itself, as does the bladder. Pupils dilate; the skin perspires. Some faces flush while others go white—either way, blood has its way with the flesh.

Fight or flight. Like we learned in science class back in high school. The body as a hunted rabbit, our animal parts, truer than we like to admit.

Amygdala. Cortisol. Adrenaline. A cocktail of chemicals. Such marvelous engineering, such spectacular simplicity. Something startles the body. A barking dog. Clap of thunder. A spider dangling over the bed. The breath catches, the heart thumps, and our vision tunnels so that we see only what's immediately before us, making the next step instantly and stunningly clear.

Hired to draw crowds to the falls for the American Centennial and Dominion Day in Canada, Maria Spelterini was forced to postpone her stunt because of the extraordinary heat of the fourth and the few days following. Finally, on the eighth of July, the palms of onlookers sweaty with heat and suspense, Maria started from the American side and worked her way over the gorge.

She was not the first to cross the falls. In the summer of 1859, The Great Blondin crossed, followed by a local who'd dubbed himself Signor Farini in 1860. Blondin crossed the gorge blindfolded and on stilts. Farini set his rope further down the gorge and matched Blondin's every stunt, dressing as an Irish washerwoman, carrying his machine onto the tightrope, and drawing water from the Niagara to fill it.

Others followed, resulting in a frenzy of crossings throughout the 1860s. The daredevils made their way back and forth over the gorge every summer, and only one of them ever fell to his death. The regularity of their stunts and their relatively easy success caused crowds to weary of the tightrope walkers. It turns out that there were only so many times an audience would pay to watch a man cross a deadly river gorge. But a woman. Well, a woman in a short skirt defying death was a different matter altogether.

Doesn't every child test her feet along the edges, learning to balance along a narrow strip of rock, a line of low fence posts, a series of old stumps in her grandmother's backyard? Watch as the child does this. Notice the body pointing itself as it moves along, the whole of it pushing into the task, the way without thinking the child lifts her arms out to the side for balance, grows herself some wings.

Courage. From the Old French *cuer* and the Latin *cor* for heart. Fathearted, it means mettle and moxie. Whether applied to solo journeys to new lands, attempts at love, or the crossing of one of the most dangerous river gorges in the world—courage requires a mix of bravery and foolishness so that the two naturally hang together.

But what's the opposite of courage? It should be cowardice, the lion holding his tail at the gates of Oz. But cowardice is its own quality, the ongoing thinning of the heart. No, the opposite of courage is not a lack of courage but something else. The prolonged choosing of comfort perhaps. Lining one's nest with excessive feathers. How to be courageous with a remote control in hand, how to try for the sky with feet that have fallen asleep?

I admire fearlessness in women, if only because it so rarely lies open.

Of course, it's there, our strength. Women rise each morning to begin again, no matter the many mouths opening in their direction, no matter the dullness or sharpness of the task. Women understand how to overlook or wait until next time, can spend years holding their tongues in the face of the thing that most wants letting. No, I need no convincing of the strength of women, but it's too often a matter of restraint. I do not often see us standing bold or brazen before a crowd. I do not mean to belittle cheerleaders and fashion models and television weather women—though theirs seems a case of the body going through a series of prescribed and pleasant motions. But where are our wild women? Those with open mouths and muscled legs, whose actions shock, whose bodies defy gravity, whose every step rivets the eye so that we can't look away?

In stereocard images of Maria's July 12 crossing, peach baskets have been strapped to her feet. An odd choice for footwear, awkward as thumbs for every toe. But when a daredevil is shown to be too capable and the crowds are no longer entranced, he or she must ratchet up the act—a meal cooked and served midway, a grown man carried on the walker's back, moving one's hips in time to the music for a waltz over the river, or peach baskets bearing the name of a local orchard for shoes.

Maria continues to mesmerize the crowds. Word spreads and people keep coming, paying their dollars and boarding trains to the falls. On July 19, she crosses blindfolded. On the twenty-second, her wrists and ankles are manacled. And on the twenty-sixth of July 1976, Maria Spelterini crosses the Niagara River Gorge a final time.

There were others. Female daredevils. Women whose acts were so bold they tempted the devil himself, nineteenth-century women and girls who challenged death for the pleasure of a crowd.

The daughter of a Norwegian circus performer and a Danish horseman, Elvira Madigan took up trick riding. Hanging from the side of a galloping horse and standing in the saddle was a risky, though standard, circus act. The walking of wires was more dangerous, but eventually, Elvira mastered the tightrope. Were it not for her tragic death at the hands of her married lover, the Danish beauty might have eventually attempted the falls herself.

Bird Millman epitomized elegance as she flitted on delicate strands. In a photograph of her high-wire act, Bird picks her way across a wire between skyscrapers with the smoke stacks of New York City at her feet. Soft and white, parasol in hand, Bird tiptoes the wire as if strolling along a boardwalk on holiday.

Zazel was fourteen years old when she was shot from a cannon in London in 1877. The first-ever human cannonball, the girl could not comfort herself with stories of earlier success. A girl launched into the air, a child made into a bullet. Zazel curled against the cool metal barrel, heart thumping against her ribcage as she waited for the launch—or perhaps at fourteen and loaded inside a metal cylinder, the girl had already arrived at the place where trembling was a luxury.

What about the rest of us?

Those of us who stick to crosswalks and curfews and submit to regular cholesterol testing. How to keep from the numbing lull of comfort? How to fly, just for a time, no matter the various bodies of water swirling beneath our feet?

In certain dreams, I fly. It's rare, especially as the years pile like spent pennies around me. Flying dreams have been usurped by dreams of the exaggerated ordinary: unending staff meetings, phone messages deleted with a wayward swipe, moving about in rooms that no longer exist—no, the flying does not come so often anymore, but when it does, I wake from the dream buoyed, as if I'd spent the night careening with the clouds.

Flying dreams are not so unusual. Like dreams of being chased and losing teeth or reporting to work buck-naked, many people have dreamed of taking to the air. My flight dreams come down to pushing my arms behind me, palms flattening into rudders, the bottoms of my feet brushing the crowns of trees, taking in a patchwork of rooftops and backyards as I rise.

I fly south, following the Genesee River toward the Allegheny, and is there anything sweeter than the sight of foothills at night? I soar over Route 390, following the highway to the Letchworth Gorge, the slate ledges and five-hundred-foot falls, the river snaking below. It's here, high above Letchworth, that I become aware of what I'm doing, the impossibility of it all, and say to myself, *Well look at this, I'm flying.*

Which is how it ends. The weight of practicality proves too much even for dreams, and I begin to sink, arms flailing, wondering where I might land and whether I will ever again make it into the sky.

Little is known of Maria Spelterini outside of her stunts. She's said to have been born on the shore of the Ligurian Sea, where she began performing with her father's troupe at the age of three, balancing on balls and beams and eventually slack wire and tightrope. She made headlines crossing ropes in Moscow, Vienna, Saint Aubin, Portugal, and Spain. Upon her arrival in America, she strung a wire and practiced in Jones's Wood in New York City, so by the time she'd arrived at Niagara, the young woman was a seasoned pro.

Reporters admired the way she combined courage with grace. The ladies at the International Hotel, where she stayed, were so taken with Maria, they presented her with the gift of a watch upon her leaving.

Given her role and her costume, it could not have been easy to charm both the men and the women of the falls, but even off her rope, Maria seems to never have made a false step. In at least one review, it's suggested that she might have fared even better with the crowds had she allowed herself a slip or two to prolong the sense of danger, or at least acted from time to time afraid.

Antidotes to fear: Saint Benedict's medal. Rosary beads. Tiny green pills. Self-help books, yoga, mantras repeated seventeen times a day. A rabbit's foot. Crucifixes and prayer shawls. Holy water and saints' bones. Glass eyes, the hamsa, and ruby pendants. The Italian horn, *il cornicello*. A bracelet strung with chalcedony and red jasper. Painted pebbles, gris-gris bags, and alligator's teeth.

In my last flying dream, I had company: my sister Stephanie. We wore long white dresses like we did back in 1976, the bicentennial, the year that in a fit of patriotic fervor, our mother shellacked a bald eagle onto our coffee table. But in the dream, a hundred years after Maria's act, we were simply two girls in peasant dresses pushing ourselves up with our thoughts, brides of the sky, flying to escape a man on our heels, a man hiking the river in untied army boots. Perhaps he was fear, that man with open shoes, the devil himself, whose hooves did not allow for the proper fastening of footwear. It was spring in the dream, and we held hands, our dresses billowing like bedsheets as we landed. The fruit of mayapples hid under tiny green umbrellas, but we knew it was there, the fruit, and that it mattered somehow. We also knew that the man approached and would reach us, but not for a moment or two, so we sailed toward the river in our dresses, heads falling back with laughter, nothing mattering so much as the moment of soaring and the field of green reaching out to receive us.

Maria Spelterini disappeared after her final crossing at the falls.

Nothing remains of her beyond newspaper accounts of her stunts and a few images. A stray report from Buffalo a few weeks after she left tells of a manager making off with her earnings. A rumor of her in South America. Her name on various lists of Niagara Falls daredevils. But no one really knows what happened to her after the summer of 1876, and she is nothing so much as a stray thread of history.

I've tried to cultivate many charms—how fine it would be to carry a source of protection, an object to embolden me. Some have been gifts: a tiny sack of worry dolls from Guatemala; a pewter Virgin Mary carved so thin, the slab of marble into which she's planted seems lush by contrast; a South African coin from a student, kept at my desk.

I have collected pebbles from a California cove, purple rocks from a fishing village in Cape Breton, a wing-shaped shell from a beach in southern France. Things of the natural world, mainly, though at times of heightened desperation, I've attempted to purchase amulets: a tiny Lady of Lourdes medal set into a necklace of sterling and pearl, a locket into which I've placed a smooth green pebble. Recently I've had my eye on a dragon pendant. Smaller than a dime, the dragon hangs from a slip of silver. I let myself imagine what it might feel like to run a finger over a creature so delicate it might break, contemplating the tender weight of ferocity.

My guess is that Maria married a farmer from Cleveland or a railroad worker from Erie, trading in Spelterini for another name: Nowicki, Corcoran, or Palumbo.

It's possible she returned to Europe and simply chose never to perform again, or maybe she did perform, in Brazil or Moscow, and there's no record of her feats—that seems unlikely however, given her appeal to the press and her many successes.

What remains is the image of her over the gorge, the plumes of hair and cloth, a young woman electrifying the air each time she stepped into it, which she did again and again before coming down from the clouds and vanishing forever.

My last attempt at securing a charm was the purchase of a *maneki neko*, the fortune cat figurine found in Chinese restaurants, nail salons, and places where pots of lucky bamboo flourish. An emblem of luck. I found a miniature version and dangled him from the volume dial in my car, where he lasted a week before falling under the seat sometime last autumn. It was a long winter, but a few days ago, he rolled out from under my driver's seat. I held the metal cat in my hands and closed my eyes, as if invoking something, before wiping him off and returning him to his dial.

Could he change anything, my little charm? And what exactly needed changing? My days are not lackluster so much as ordinary, the price we pay for growing up. Perhaps the problem is not my tendency toward caution at all but wanting too much from this life. And what could he do anyway, that little cat? Remind me of how much I enjoyed the idea of flying, help me to be more daring?

All I know is that when I joined my husband on a hike later that day, a golden bird flew from the stump of a cypress tree.

I'm not one to search for birds, preferring instead to let them simply cross my path. But I like to wander with those who do, and this bird was different. Once known as a golden swamp warbler, the bird is now called a prothonotary warbler—named for Roman Catholic officials, the *protonotarii*, whose gold robes match the birds' plumage. Something about its color and obscurity captivated me, and I'd been hoping for a glimpse of one for years.

On this day, we walked a boardwalk over wetlands in east Arkansas, the platform populated by fishermen whose buckets of night crawlers and pickup trucks seemed worlds away from our binoculars and hybrid automobile. But we approached anyway, and as we did, one of them called out a welcome.

"Y'all looking for a little bird?" he asked and pointed to the place where he'd seen something earlier. We nodded and followed, and just like that, a golden bird. Tiny thing, making a nest of fishing wire and Arkansas mud. We tiptoed to the edge of the dock, but need not have done so because the warbler flew without caution from his stump into the new green of cypress needles, gathering old leaves and going on with his business, despite the nearness of fishermen and binoculars and footsteps.

How brave, I thought. Or something close to brave, but less of a choice, that quality in certain creatures that knows fear but does not abide it. The reclusive warbler, the world encroaching into his swamp, the ever-present possibility of fishhook and cowbird and cottonmouth.

That a little bird, flitting gold and doing what birds must do—flying and flying straight into the face of the world.

The child's handlers claimed she was found in the jungles of Southeast Asia in the early 1880s, though so many false statements were made about the girl, it's hard to trust any source. What is most certain is that Krao Farini was exhibited as Darwin's missing link (conveniently just after Darwin's death), and while not wholly endorsed as such by science, the claim was taken seriously enough for crowds to gather around the girl during the late nineteenth century.

HUMAN CURIOSITY

A CIRCULAR CONCORDANCE

CEMETERY, A SCENE: Now to Saint Michael's, where the sideshow has set up camp, a parade of irregular shadows stretching toward the grave. The Giant from Texas carries in his own chair to be sure he'll fit somewhere, while the Fat Lady heaps praises on the deceased and the Leopard-Skin Girl grieves beside the casket, the spots on her flesh rising and falling as she weeps. April 1926. The air swells with the scent of lilies and funeral roses, all of Astoria perfumed as the congregants gather round—the Sword-Swallowers and the Human Pincushions and ladies with tattoos blooming on the trellises of their flesh.

Abide with me, they sing. *Lead kindly light.*

DIRGE: [dûrj] *n.*
   1. Music
      a. A funeral hymn or lament.
      b. A slow, mournful musical composition.
   2. A mournful or elegiac poem or other literary work.
   3. Roman Catholic Church: The office of the dead.
Origin: 1175–1225; Middle English Latin variant of dĭrige, first word of the antiphon sung in the Latin office of the dead

BENEDICTION: "Krao," her friends cry to the casket. Their hearts leak for the loss of their darling, the "peacemaker of the sideshow," "the best-liked of freaks."

ORIGINS OF THE GIRL: As many stories were told about Krao's origins as the rumors swirling about the peculiarities of the girl's body—cheek pouches, they claimed. Hair growing like a mane between her shoulder blades. A hidden tail.

Rescued from the monkey-people of Burma, some said.

Stolen from the jungles of Siam.

She was reported to speak a few words of Malay and was rumored to feed herself with her toes.

Burma or *Bangkok*. People spoke of the girl as if paying their quarters to see her gave them access to the facts. But no one knew for sure where she came from, and the seven-year-old could have been lifted from a tenement in Brooklyn as easily as from the branches of a temple tree in Thailand.

ORIGIN OF THE SPECIES: Charles Darwin's groundbreaking work in evolutionary biology, published in 1859. Darwin contradicted the existing biblically based creation story, shocking readers with his claim that humans evolved from a common ancestor to apes. Such talk titillated the masses, and his work was widely read. People paid to attend lectures by self-described scientists who highlighted the more sensational aspects of Darwin's theory, working people into a lather over the idea of a missing link between humans and apes.

MISSING LINK:

1. A theoretical primate postulated to bridge the evolutionary gap between the anthropoid apes and humans.
   (No longer in scientific use.)
2. Something lacking but needed to complete a series.

HUMAN CURIOSITY: The Victorians flocked to see legless acrobats and conjoined twins, making entertainment of human oddities, making dime museums and sideshows all the rage. How they came to stare, the London throngs, eyes arriving miles before their feet, offering up coins, well-dressed ladies clamoring to see the child pull wedges of fruit from the pouches of her cheeks. Even those who were not ordinarily seduced came to see Krao. An oddity, yes, but the child was important science, living proof of Darwin's claims.

MORPHOLOGY:

The head and low forehead are covered down to the bushy eyebrows with the deep black, lank, and lusterless hair, characteristic of the mongoloid races. The whole body is also overgrown with a far less dense coating of soft, black hair about a quarter of an inch long, but nowhere close enough to conceal the color of the skin which may be described as of a dark olive-brown shade. The nose is extremely short and low, with excessively broad nostrils, merging in the full pouched cheeks, into which she appears to have the habit of stuffing her food, monkey-fashion. Like those of the anthropoids, her feet are also prehensile, and the hands so flexible that they bend quite back over the wrists. The thumb also doubles completely back, and of the four fingers, all the top joints bend at pleasure independently inward. Prognathism seems to be very slightly developed, and the beautiful round black eyes are very large and perfectly horizontal. Hence, the expression is, on the whole, far from unpleasing.

From "Krao, The Human Monkey," *New York Times*, February 8, 1883

FREAK MERCHANT: *n.*

One who specializes in the acquisition and marketing of human oddities.

(see also Farini, William).

FARINI, WILLIAM: Born William Hunt in Lockport, New York, Hunt relocated with his family to Ontario, Canada, when he was a child. As a young man, Hunt resisted and eventually abandoned the trappings of his provincial beginnings and rechristened himself Guillermo Farini. An adventurer, Farini took to the tightrope. He trained himself to perform and crossed the falls at Niagara, making Farini a successful daredevil in his own right before he moved on to work as an inventor and manager of other acts, eventually becoming a successful promoter and peddler of human curiosities.

CURIOSITY: [ky*oo*r-ee-OS-i-tee] *n.*

1. A desire to know or learn.
2. A desire to know about people or things that do not concern one; nosiness.

3. An object that arouses interest, by being novel or extraordinary.

4. A strange or odd aspect.

5. Archaic, Fastidiousness.

[Origin: Fourteenth century, Middle English *curiosite*, from Old French and Latin]

VENUES: The Royal Aquarium in London. Audiences with gentlemen, scientists, and European nobility. Sellout crowds in America, the Consolidated Monster Show, Barnum's American Museum.

MARKETING: Farini gave the child his last name, taught her bits of German and French, and showed her how to play the piano. He called himself her father and wanted to educate the girl, but more than anything, Farini understood the delicious contradiction of ornamenting his hairy child with fine dresses and courtly manners. Krao Farini, he called her, then trumpeted the girl as Darwin's missing link. Star attraction and adopted daughter, Farini and Krao traveled together throughout Europe and North America for years before the ever-adventurous Farini moved on to other attractions; the Lost City of the Kalahari, talking walruses, and the intensive study of begonias.

OUTCOME: But even the best of shows must come to an end. Eventually the crowds dwindled, and the girl looked up one day and found that she was a woman. The public had had their fill of Darwin, and the man who'd always marketed her had moved on. Farini eventually took up the role of gentleman, learned to paint with oils, and aligned himself with minor nobles, leaving the sideshow and flying trapeze far behind him. But Krao did not quit—even if she'd wanted to, what else would she have done? The sideshow circuit is what she knew best, the exchange of money for the privilege of open staring. Krao hid behind veils on the New York streets, but during working hours, she allowed the stares, eventually landing the role of bearded lady at Coney Island.

SIDESHOW BOOTH, A VIEW FROM INSIDE: Faces loom like moons, swarm of mouth and tongue, *ooh* and *ah* and *do you see that?* Sometimes too, a hand, fingers pointing as the line pushes past, staring as long as they can, willing themselves to remember every strand, making the most of each and every cent. *Mama, look at the hairy lady*, and the children you almost don't mind, but here comes a lady who remembers, one from way back when, her body beginning to fold under the burden of fine clothes, hair piled under a hat, one of her sort comes by more than you'd expect—*Tell me, darling Krao, do you still stash wedges of orange in your cheek?* The knife of familiarity in the voice, as if you had attended her wedding, as if you knew the names of her children—*Can you still reach your ear with a toe, sweet Krao?* Men are quiet at least, lewd sometimes, wanting to see under the clothes, once or twice a day one of them saying, *Well, I'll be.* The line moves on, eyes swimming like so many fish, the crush of skin white as coconut flesh, crunch of popcorn, stench of sugar, the painted lips and the tongue again, running pink over a row of sticky teeth.

KRAO: Not a name so much as an animal sound. Rhyme of *ow*, relative in sound to *growl* and *howl*, as in a yelp of pain. Krao. A name conjured by Farini, perfect for a creature linking man to chimp. A word for posters and pamphlets. But the child had a name, didn't she, one given by her mother before she was taken or sold, a name she might have said to herself while people stared, a few syllables invoked like armor or said like a prayer before sleep, whispering as she let herself into bed—rubbing it like oil upon the inner wrist, the most tender stretch of flesh.

POSSIBILITIES, A FEW: *Kulap* means rose; *Phueng* is little bee. She might have been called *Lawan* (beautiful). It's possible Krao remembered the taste of curried fish, the texture of banana flowers. She may have seen plumerias in bloom, may have known the warmth of being held, or the wonder of the body not remarked upon. It's possible she was once called flower, once given the name beautiful, once spoken of as a tiny winged thing.

TEMPLE TREE: [*Plumeria rubra*] A deciduous plant, native to Mexico, Central and South America, widely cultivated in tropical climates worldwide. Popular in gardens and parks, the tree is often planted near temples and cemeteries. It can grow to twenty feet. Fragrant flowers unfold in shades of pink, white, and yellow from the branches. In Southeast Asia, its flowers are used as religious offerings, to ornament altars and coffins. As for herself, Krao did not want a coffin. She wanted to be finally free of the body and the gaping but failed to put her request for cremation in writing. So it was a coffin when she died, her body eventually lowered into the ground.

CEMETERY SCENE, A BRIEF RETURN: Here they come again, a parade of strange shadows encircling the grave. The Sword-Swallowers and the Fat Ladies and the Giant with his king-sized chair, weeping for Krao's kindness, his trememndous heart breaking for the one who was so sweet.

She might have been called Little Bee, might have known the glory of temple trees erupting into bloom over her head, must have harbored a thousand secrets, but all that's left is the image of her friends crowding stone angels at Saint Michael's, the chorus of them raising their voices in song.

Jerusalem the golden, with milk and honey blest, sing her friends, men and women of such unusual contour and proportion, it's possible the tears they cry are not for Krao alone:

I know not, oh, I know not, what joys await us there.

What radiancy of glory, what bliss beyond compare.

A breeze comes over the place, chilling the Leopard-Skin Girl as she lowers her head to bid a final good-bye to Krao. A girl bought and sold. A body people paid to glimpse, to study, and to stare. But for all the looking, she was hardly ever seen.

The Freaks wipe away the last of their tears. The Giant heaves his chair into the air as they turn back toward the sideshow, back to their various cages and booths, walking slowly as they move, noticing perhaps the way the trees in Astoria have begun to bud, the lilacs and viburnum, pushing their new teeth out into the world.

Kate Chopin is best known for her stories about Creole society from the upper-class white point of view. "Beyond the Bayou" was first published for children and shows the postwar plantation from the former slave La Folle's experience. All italicized text (except the line Il était lourd?) is taken directly from Chopin's story.

THE SECOND MORNING

Was he heavy, La Folle? That boy you carried? The one whose face you conjured while setting *croquinoles* into spattering oil, fixing his favorite treat—your one and only Chéri. When he visited this morning, he'd insisted on shooting squirrel for your supper, an act of love: *One squirrel ain't a bite. I'll bring you mo' 'an one, La Folle.*

An overproud child with a mission and a gun—never a good combination. Still a surprise though, the pop of gun and his voice, hurt and calling out.

Was he heavy as you ran with him through the stand of sweet gum trees, roots tangled like snakes at your feet?

What care must be taken with such boys. How tender the hearts of children who make gifts of squirrel and hair—for he gave you his hair as well. I too was once given a boy's hair. He was a middle-school child; I was his teacher. He came to my desk and handed over the packet: blue-black hair tied with red ribbon. I stared into the strands, baffled and ashamed, and later pushed them into the soil surrounding an orange tree, La Folle—a grove of miniature trees kept at my windowsill for the best part of a certain year. And your boy, when he presented you with the gift of newly cut curls, they were tied with a red ribbon just the same, but you wouldn't have buried it—you whose home was rife with water moccasins and snapping turtles would not have been troubled by the rough truth of human hair. You would have hung Chéri's curls near the window of your cabin. You might have thought it the best thing in the world, curls from the boy you loved best, the one for whom you crossed the line.

But we've reached the point where you're about to leave the bayou, La Folle, so I should call you by your Christian name—Jacqueline—a beautiful name, and you know better than I the importance of names and what we continue to allow ourselves to be called. You must know too that you can never squeeze back into a cage from which you've sprung. Strange, the longing for that which once contained us. But I jump ahead, for we are only just now on the threshold. For now you're still La Folle, the madwoman, called so for your refusal to leave your cabin and the unplanted field beside it—all while living close to a place called Bellissime, the most beautiful plantation.

Scaredy-cat, La Folle.

It started in the war, the sight of P'tit Maître covered in black powder and blood. You were just a bitty girl, and the sight of all that blood made you lose your mind with fear of the world beyond your door. (But was it really so crazy, La Folle, to fear the world given the blood, the war, North and South, and the color of your skin?)

Thirty years have come and gone, practically your whole life. The boy you saw bloodied is now grown and married—master of the plantation, father to the one whose sweetness slays you. Thirty years. But you remain in the snug trap of your cabin, with its patches of cotton, corn, and tobacco, the cows that sometimes amble over when the bayou is low. You have your habits, your joys—Master's son is your favorite. You love those little white girls, his sisters, but Maître's boy, Chéri, strokes your dark hand and lays his head on your knee. Or at least he did, for he shows less affection these days, now that he's grown tall and got himself a gun.

Still, he comes to visit. You make him cakes, and he stuffs his pockets with treats swiped from the table at the big house, almonds and raisins, then goes off with his gun to find some squirrels, which brings us back to the shot splitting the quiet of your cabin.

Your body starts, making its way over the strip of cotton to the woods to find Chéri, heart ratcheting as you lift the child and push through the abandoned field, no time for thought at all until you reach the edge of your world; the bayou and the line you've never crossed.

What can be done, La Folle?

He's only shot himself a little bit and will not die, but the child is frightened and bleeding, the face you see is his father's from long ago—blood and gun powder—you begin to shake, calling him *mon bebe* while standing at the edge of everything and crying out for his father: *Oh, P'tit Maitre! P'tit Maitre! Venez donc! Au secours! Au secours!*

But no one hears. No one comes. The boy is crying; your feet are locked beside a live oak, the only witness to your calling. Except for me, of course, the reader, whose breath grows shallow as I watch the dread make its way into each and every one of your cells—remembering how you stood in this very spot when your old mistress died, wailing and doubled over in grief. You could not cross to bid her good-bye; you could not cross for all those years, until this very moment. Until this very morning.

Now, with Chéri in your arms, you push through.

The bayou is dry, and you cross and follow a footpath you've never seen, flying under a canopy of tupelo and black willow. You're a work of fiction, Jacqueline, but truer than anything else as you run under those trees, wanting to fall to the ground with fear but running anyway, even as you call out to God for mercy, *Bon Dieu, ayez pitie La Folle! Bon Dieu, ayez pitie moi!* The writer of the story guides you all the way to the big house, allowing you to fall only after delivering Chéri into his daddy's arms.

You wake once again inside your cabin. A new morning. And this is where I want to push my hand through the page to track you beyond the reach of ink. The second morning. After the rising action. After you've passed through the night, accompanied by friends gathered round with herbs and proclamations of death, after the panic of the previous day. You do not die. You love that boy but do not pay for it with your life. Instead, you rise with *the first touch of cool gray morning*, put on a new dress, and leave the bayou once again.

This time, your stride is steady as you step beyond the bayou. It's dawn, and the fields of cotton become as if silver; the song of birds everywhere. Indigo buntings, tanagers with scarlet feathers. The waxen bells of magnolias, *and the jessamine clumps . . . and roses too.*

You walk on. Up the veranda, where your knock is answered by Chéri's mother, who hides her surprise at seeing you once again beyond the bayou. She reports her son's health and suggests that you come back to see him when he wakes, but you say, *Non, madame. I'm goin' wait yair tell Chéri wake up.* And the way you say it, La Folle:

Non, madame.

We're meant to be impressed by your love for the boy, meant to admire your determination to be certain he's well, and we do—I do—but how can I not hear it?

Non, madame.

Surely some new madness has entered your head, so certain are the words to Chéri's mother in your unwavering patois. She loves you for carrying her son to safety, and we hear the benevolence in her voice:

Ah, La Folle! Is it you, so early?

It's a beautiful story, and you, a character the writer created to show that where fear is great, love must be greater. It's a true enough lesson, of course, so that I almost believe it's what to take from the story—and had Chéri's mother called you *Jacqueline,* it might have been enough. But she calls you La Folle. She does not see that you've changed, that you can never again be La Folle. Even if love allowed you to cross that line the first time, something else guided you the second time, and Chéri's mother, benevolent or not, is a white woman in nineteenth-century Louisiana, and nothing breaks in your voice as you tell her no, nothing trembles as you make yourself comfortable on her porch, setting your hands onto long legs, leaning into the rising sun as you wait shimmering in the new day.

That should be enough.

Kate Chopin leaves you waiting on the porch, presumably for the sight of Chéri and the security that will come when you see that all is right. She leaves you with the implied conclusion of health for Chéri and freedom for you, and I should do the same. Only I can't turn away from the story that starts on the last page, on the second morning, freedom becoming its own question as you stretch into the sun like it's the first sun ever come. What do you think as you sit beholding gardens, the confetti of crape myrtles and stone goddesses locked in poses, the magnolia lit with new light? Do you see it yet, the way your little cabin and the sound of Chéri's voice will never be enough now that the cotton has grown pretty? A hard miracle of the body. Once it's tackled a line that kept it in place, it loses the ability to be satisfied to stand behind others.

So tell me, Jacqueline, *Il était lourd?*

Was he heavy, that boy?

And now you've set him down, what will you do with those newly strong arms?

And now, a dark-haired girl in a yellow dress, a classmate I barely knew,

a child I shouldn't remember and hardly do, outside of the dress and

the hair and half smile, all of which have survived over thirty years.

ROSALIE, FROM
THE PHILIPPINES

They are twins, the girls in my class. One blonde, the other brunette, faces pointed at the chin, bony noses, oversized eyes. One is named Laverne or has a name close to Laverne—Lavinda or Lavonne. But to me, she's Laverne, and it's nothing short of cruelty that her dark-haired sister is not named Shirley, is not named at all, in fact, is nothing but shadow and head-nodder to the other girl, lodged forever in memory as the wrongly named twin to Laverne.

Both girls sport choppy shags, and with the shortish hair and angled faces, they look a bit like boys. Their matching clothes are not so unusual really—matching is to be expected with twins—but the outfits themselves are odd. One-piece coveralls like race-car drivers wear, jumpsuits studded with shoulder stripes and patches bearing the names of tire companies and motor oil. Only the color of their jumpsuits differs. Laverne in the orange stands close to me, with her sister in blue at her sleeve.

How strange these sisters, dressed like a pit-stop crew and hovering at my side, but what isn't strange? I'm the new girl and as the other children file out the door to line up for another class, music or art, the sisters crowd me near the coat closet, asking what school I came from while instructing me in the ways of the classroom. I listen, eyes wide, trying to take in every last thing:

Put spelling quizzes here.

Monday is music day.

Akron, as in Ohio?

Somewhere inside the closet, a girl rifles through her things, the sound of paper and zipper in the background. Laverne rolls her eyes when she sees me look toward the girl whose yellow dress is puckered at the bodice and dotted with flowers.

"That's just Rosalie," she says, lowering her voice as the girl passes. "She's from the Philippines."

"We don't talk to her," Shirley chimes in, delighted to contribute. "She's so ugly."

I look again at the girl who has just left the coat closet, and it's as if someone has lifted the school building and shaken it, leaving me to lurch inside the cinder-block walls, reaching out to steady myself as everything is in motion. My family had lived on the reservation near Buffalo with kids whose skin was soft brown and where girls who looked like Rosalie were the best any of us could hope for, a place where pale skin was pitied, light hair considered unfortunate. Except for the clean cotton dress that looks like it came from another era, a time when girls wore dresses and boys long sleeves and ties—except for the dress and the kinky bends of her hair—Rosalie looks so like the kids I'd just left that I nearly follow as she steps out into the hall. But no, I don't follow. Instead, I face the jump-suited sisters, wondering if I'd heard wrong.

"What?" I mumble. "What did you say?"

The teacher's voice cuts into my question and sends the three of us skittering into the hall where the rest of the class waits. I take my place behind Rosalie in the line of black and white faces, wondering if there's something special about the Philippines, something I'm supposed to know. I stare into the swath of dark hair and think again of the reservation, the way we'd left without warning, the toys and clothes and old photographs abandoned when we packed into the car that day—anything that wouldn't fit between elbows and knees thrown into a field of milkweed and sedge. I think of this and the way things come and go, the way nothing stands still for very long, then look back into Rosalie's hair, seeing in it something of my closest sister, the dark waves I've always wanted. I think of prettiness and ugliness too—what the words mean and how quickly even the most solid definitions can change.

She turns around then, Rosalie, and gives a smile, out of politeness or because she feels the weight of my staring. Her smile is quick and small, and I return it, and it's almost a tender moment, except that she's not there the following day or the following week, and in any case, all trace of Rosalie disappears before we have a chance to become friends.

"Back to the Philippines probably," Laverne says when I ask about Rosalie during lunch. "And no one misses her," she adds, jutting the ridge of her chin toward the table, indicating where to sit.

I'm not asked for my opinion, nor do not give it. My clothes are hand-me-downs and I don't yet speak up, but I want to tell them that I know something of beauty. I would like to take my tray of food and move to the empty end of the table. I'd love to float to the ceiling and hover above the cafeteria, glide out of the long rectangle of school, sweep the length of the city until I found Rosalie in her 1950s church dress and let myself fall from the sky and land beside her, where the two of us would share a book.

Instead, I keep quiet while starting on my lunch and learn firsthand what happens to words not said in third grade, the way they stay with you, their weight doubling with the years, so that, at times, I find myself caught inside the memory of Laverne and Shirley and Rosalie, as if the decades have not come and gone. I'm there, in the grade-school cafeteria, wedged between the sisters and their matching plastic lunchboxes, chewing back words most in need of speaking, while around me, a new world slides into place.

In nineteenth-century Kentucky, a family became carriers of a rare blood condition that rendered the skin of some of its members blue. Though most of the family did not show blue, those who did were known as the "Blue Fugates" before the disorder was eliminated by modern medicine and the influx of new settlers (and new blood) into the region.

BLUE KENTUCKY GIRL

Named for the moon. Little Luna. Luna, blue. The details surrounding her birth are murky; some say 1878, while others say a decade later. But why squabble over a handful of years? By the time she was born in eastern Kentucky, people had settled into its isolated pockets, inhabiting hollows along the Cumberland Plateau, fringed by rocky ridges and ravines. Men cut timber and women tended children and planted corn and potatoes wherever they could clear rocks; the hardness of their lives contrasted with a backdrop bursting with waterfall and fern. Into this world, little ones came, eventually replacing fathers and mothers; they were boys and girls for the shortest of time. One of them came near the end of the century, a girl born into the Fugate family, the one I call to now, little Luna blue.

Luna's mama would have been raised on stories of Fugates going back to the time Troublesome Creek was settled in the 1820s. She would have known a few of her husband's strangely tinted cousins, would have spent time with an indigo-skinned niece. She'd married a Fugate after all, and in the isolated hills of eastern Kentucky, there was so much intermarriage that even she carried a spot of Fugate blood. *The Blue People of Kentucky*, the Fugates were known for miles.

But what could that have to do with Luna's mother, Mahala, whose skin was white, as was her husband's and all her other babies', each of whom unfolded from her body soft and pink as azalea blossoms?

You would think that skin color couldn't matter when you're white in a country that prizes whiteness, but of course, it sometimes does, not only for blue people but for pink ones too. So much is relative to setting, and I was never so white as the summer we lived on the reservation, the fall and winter too. I never wanted anything so much as to be brown skinned because of how pretty the color and because I didn't like to stand out. Later, when we moved to the city, I continued to covet the skin of those around me, Puerto Rican and black girls, families from Laos who'd been resettled by local churches, even the faintly olive hue of Italian girls. To be cracker and honky can be a lonely business depending on where you live. It's a good lesson, perhaps, the white child forced to face the precarious hierarchy of the flesh. But for the shy among us, the retiring, how lovely the prospect of looking like those we like best.

Most babies born with Fugate blood were as pale as every other white child in eastern Kentucky. Even those who showed a tinge upon birth usually lost their color after a few weeks, a fact Mahala might have clung to as she cradled Luna, whose skin was like a stain against her breast. Families had to scrounge to survive in those hills, and Mahala couldn't have afforded much time to worry—though when was being different ever courted? Life was hard enough without the burden of strange skin. Mahala must have lifted the edge of her blanket to check on Luna again and again, listening hard to those around her, repeating to herself the cluck of old aunts and her husband's reassurances.

Just give it time, they'd say, *that young'un's skin will right itself, fade as fast as the passing of days.*

The days passed and passed again, but Luna remained the bluest of all babies born at Troublesome Creek, blue as the gentians growing along the river, blue as the berries that come in summer, blue as the moon hanging like a lantern in the night sky.

A blue moon isn't as rare as it might seem. Two full moons in one month, it happens once—sometimes twice—a year. *Once in a blue moon.* The saying began as a way to speak not so much of a rarity but of absurdity, such as hell freezing over, raining cats and dogs, or the features of a girl's face the color of denim patches her mama sewed on her daddy's torn trousers. *Once in a blue moon,* they say, and mean *hardly ever.* Then along came you.

Commonly known as met-H, methaemoglobinaemia is a disorder resulting in the reduced ability to carry oxygen in the blood, so that the blood of those affected becomes so dark, it tints the skin blue, a condition known as cyanosis, or "blue disease." The condition is usually caused by environmental factors, reactions to certain drugs, or exposure to nitrates and dyes. In rare cases, however, blue skin is congenital, as in the case of the Fugates, whose randomly aligned alleles combined with chance and geographic isolation to produce blue people in Troublesome Creek for more than one hundred years.

There are so many blues in Kentucky. The heads of grasses. Music, the picking and the banjos, voices singing out from the lonesome hills. The moon, looming large in the sky, making the night its very own shade. A moon sung of by Bill Monroe and again by Patsy Cline and Elvis—the boy who sang another song about the blue moon—and that should be enough. That should be plenty, but there's Kentucky's best-known daughter, Loretta Lynn, who came from a hollow not too far from Luna's and who reached out to her love, singing, *Come on back,* her voice sad and strong in "Blue Kentucky Girl."

Blue as a bruise, they said of the lips on Luna Fugate's face.
Blue all over. As blue a woman as I ever saw.

Mr. Bose taught industrial arts, which wasn't art so much as teaching children to cut pieces of wood, to sand them smooth, and to glue them into useful objects. He was missing a finger or two, which contradicted his claims of safety regarding the band saw, and he'd flip his lid from time to time when someone couldn't remember how to use a ruler after he'd showed us ten times. I tried to keep out of his way, noticing what set him off and showing I could count inches and cut wood, though I was in truth afraid of the blade. Imagine my surprise when he yanked away my project one day. I'd used too much paint, it turns out, slathering my wooden paper dispenser in thick layers of white and dotting it with pink flowers as if it were a wedding cake. Mr. Bose snatched it up and took it to the sink, ran it under the faucet, and went on a tirade about wasted paint while milky water splattered everywhere.

One day, after someone said something about race, saying *spic* or *cracker*—maybe *Oreo* or *zebra*—he threw down the level he was holding, letting it clatter to the floor, and demanded we power down our saws and come away from our vice grips. He yanked a few large sheets of construction paper and told us to place our hands flat against pages of black, tan, peach, and white paper. We stayed there, hands extended and frozen, a circle of city kids wondering whether the teacher might be far gone enough to cut off our fingers.

"Tell me," he yelled, "which of you matches any of these colors?"

"Who here thinks he is black or white or yellow?"

"We're all in between," he said when no one answered, and we nodded, looking into our various colored faces, too scared to disagree. He held us there for a minute, our hands against the sheets of paper.

"See," he said. "None of us is any one true color."

Luna was still a girl when she was spotted by an admirer while attending services at the Baptist church. Perhaps something caught him as she sang a hymn, her voice strong and clear: *Just as I am, without one plea.*

Whatever the boy thought, it did not keep him from calling. And when they married, he built a two-room log cabin on a section of her daddy's land out in the middle of Laurel Fork Hollow. Luna's flesh could not have repelled him for he came to her, and came again, and together they filled their cabin to bursting. He cut trees while she cared for each of the babies through long days and short nights. Children grow up fast in those parts, working and singing and telling stories sometimes but learning most of all to make do.

Thirteen babies are known to have survived. There were more pregnancies, but in the end, thirteen satellites orbited Luna's moon. Did she look at their skin first thing, scanning the whole of their bodies for signs of mottling?

So much is unknown. Whether anyone came to help with the births. Whether her babies' skin had the look of thin milk. What those children thought as they grew, whether they learned to think of all mamas as blue.

All the children had flesh as white as their father's, regular as everyone they met in their part of the world and beyond, so that, even in the company of her own family, Luna remained one of a kind, leading a pack of pale-skinned children into the woods to collect ramps in spring, frying them with potatoes in bacon fat, setting and clearing the table, until everything was finished and she could rest a spell before rising to do it all again.

Blue. The feeling we have from time to time, so low, our hearts seem to have fallen into our shoes. The name given to the music of newly freed people as they tramped north over the hills and hollows, singing slow and raw as molasses, music that sweetened the strings of banjos as it made its way into the sound of the hills.

The color of morning glories. Cornflower and forget-me-nots and eyes sometimes. Royal, cobalt, and turquoise. The color of queens and kings and the Virgin's robe. Jays and buntings and cerulean warblers, whose color in the sunlight could make a grown man weep. Robins' eggs, the patina of old brass, and certain pine needles. The color of rivers and lakes. Of ocean and heaven, and faraway seas.

But here I am making pretty her life, talking up the hills of eastern Kentucky, invoking birds, speaking of wild leeks and morning glories, conjuring the majesty of early morning. There was that, of course; there must have been that. But reality must interfere: mountainsides stripped of trees, earth scraped clean, hardscrabble days, the stretching of cornmeal to fifteen mouths, buckets of water lugged up from the creek, the ice of winter seeping into broken shoes, another baby to birth, another baby to bury, men using their bodies to fell chestnuts and poplars until their legs give way like the trunks they cut into, the pennies becoming fewer, the call of mountain whiskey, the cry of the empty belly, clothes to wash and mend, the pile of things awaiting repair.

What is it about Luna that leads me to make of her a canvas?

Her life, I imagine, was plenty hard but likely no different from most everyone else's life. The name, I suppose, and the blue skin. A woman living in a place called Lonesome Creek, like and unlike everyone around her, her days tinged another shade, so that the everyday aches took on an edge, toothy and irregular, sharp as a saw blade.

I am a hundred years and many miles removed from you, Luna, but that doesn't stop me from trying to look into your face for what shows beyond the skin. To hear your voice. To understand the world as you saw it. What were the spaces like, Luna, those times between the digging of potatoes and the mending of shoes? You lived in this world for eighty-four years, so tell me what was life besides mouths to feed, squeezing into two rooms, sore bones, and nowhere to stretch? I want to know that there were times when you stopped all that motion, set hand on knee, and looked up and into the trees—times when it was just you and the dogwoods and whatever thing Jesus might mean.

Just as I am, without one plea.

That old hymn, did you sing it when you were alone? Did it ever stop being uncomfortable, being different? If you were made into a children's story or a three-part play, by the end of act 3, you'd have learned to trumpet your blue. But in real life, did you ever learn to see your difference as a gift? If you'd been in industrial arts class with me, would you have spoken up, demanded that Mr. Bose add another sheet of paper, a shade between the color of river and opal? Would you have said to the teacher what we all wanted to? *Of course we have color. Of course it matters.* The man was well intentioned. It would be nice to think there are things that others don't see, but the truth is that we are sometimes different in the face of others, the cruel beauty of the flesh.

How much I would have liked you for a partner in that elementary school class. How I would have liked to know you, if only for a day. I would have settled beside you in the crowded cafeteria and followed you outside for recess, sat at the picnic table near the old pine tree, pestering you with questions, watching as you looked up and into the clouds, taking in their volume and width—saying, *tell me, Luna, does the sky seem to you closer than kin, truer than the color of everything else?*

My Heart and I lie small upon the earth

like a grain of throbbing sand.

—ZITKALA-ŠA

THE OTHER MAGPIE

1. I will not write about the fake Indian. There's the chance that she's not fake, and trying to decide what's real becomes its own trouble. Besides, there are others to consider, my sister, for instance, who's part Seneca and will forever remind me of the fawn we found one day unfolding its legs near a little stream. Something dangling from a shrub stopped us—my husband and I always pause to watch the stream slip under the footbridge into the marsh where cattails and roses grow—swamp roses blooming pink and fine to see—but something shone from a branch, reflecting enough light to make our stopping sudden that day. A strand of green beads, from Saint Patrick's Day or Mardi Gras, had found its way to that unlikely stretch of land, tossed by a child perhaps, or dropped by a bird. Such were my thoughts when, just like that, movement near the little creek, a fawn looking as if she was making use of her legs for the first time. Something of the fawn, shivering and lovely colored, reminds me of my youngest sister. But I will not write about her either—though, as I say, she's a real Indian, and beads shining from trees when you least expect them have a way of marking a spot.

2. Neither will I linger long over Zitkala-Ša, though her image haunts me.

In a series of photographs by Gertrude Käsebier, Zitkala-Ša is posed holding first a basket, then a book, finally a violin. The objects are symbolic props. Sioux women weave baskets, and while she is of them, she has left them and learned to play violin, to write, and to inhabit the world of books.

In 1884, Zitkala-Ša and a group of other children from the Yankton Reservation in South Dakota boarded a train and traveled seven hundred miles east to White's Manual Labor Institute in Indiana. The children were promised apples, Zitkala-Ša later wrote; the missionaries had lured them with talk of orchards and red fruit. Upon arrival, their soft leather was exchanged for hard shoes and dresses of scratchy wool. They were expected to forget the language of their mothers and fathers and speak only English, forever severing them from their tribes. Leaving her mother was hard on the eight-year-old, but Zitkala-Ša was an eager student and was nearly able to stomach her losses until the day her braids were taken.

"I lost my spirit," Zitkala-Ša later wrote of that day. As an adult, her writing brought her success but also trouble at the Carlisle Indian School, where she worked and whose administrators did not want an Indian remembering out loud the pain of trying to escape scissors, the way she'd hid under a bed but they'd found her and forced the girl's submission by strapping her into a chair. No matter all that came later—photographs of her in a long white dress with puffed sleeves and floral wallpaper, looking like a bride—the image that lingers is a child bound to a chair, wildness slipping away as dark hair coils on the floor.

5. Tempting too is Catharine Montour: *Queen Catharine* of the Iroquois—as a general rule, women called *queen* are tough to resist. The daughter of a French Iroquois woman called *French Margaret* and a Mohawk known as *Peter Quebek*, Catharine married a Seneca chief, and when her husband was killed in a raid, she assumed leadership of the lush valley in south central New York State.

Used by the British during the Revolutionary War, Catharine's Town was burned to the ground in 1779 by the Sullivan expedition, which pushed through the region destroying villages as punishment for the Iroquois' aiding the English. For their part, British forces failed to protect the villagers as promised, and many froze to death or starved. Those who survived, including Catharine, pushed as far west as they could go without falling into the great river at Niagara. Though her family history was long and colorful in the region, often bridging the European and Native communities, little more is known of Catharine. And perhaps it's better to set aside our queen for a time and turn our attention to a saint.

4. How can I help but love a woman called *Lily of the Mohawks?*

Lily is likely meant in the virginal sense and not in deference to the tiger lilies growing along reservation roadsides, but I can pretend she's named for orange trumpets and remember the local church that now bears her name. I think of area Catholics, Irish and Italian Americans, praying in a church named for an Iroquois woman and want to find a statue of my Mohawk Lily, surround it in roses, and light candles at her feet.

Born in 1656 in what is now upper New York State, Kateri somehow found the strength to stand up to her tribe, steadfastly refusing marriage and eventually making her way north to a mission in New France, where she converted to Catholicism—changing her name from Tekakwitha, meaning "She who bumps into things," to Kateri, Mohawk for *Catherine,* after Catherine of Siena. A bold move for one whose vision was so impaired she *did* bump into things, a girl so modest she covered her head with a blanket.

It's impossible to think of Kateri without considering all that befell her. As a child, she'd witnessed the death of her parents and baby brother from smallpox, the same epidemic that left her scarred and half-blind, the disease that washed ashore with boatloads of Europeans. Kateri must have been lonesome, a child with no mother to convince her of the beauty beyond the scars, and I can't separate the image of the girl from the acts of self-mortification upon her conversion.

Kateri became an expert self-punisher, denying herself food, piercing her flesh, donning a belt of thorns, inflicting so much suffering on her body that even the priests became concerned. It's this she's sainted for and not her everyday losses, the bearing of which would make for thousands of Native saints. But sainthood requires miracles too, and it's said that Kateri's skin grew smooth and clear upon death, which seems the cruelest sort of trick, beauty bestowed on our Lily when it can no longer matter.

5. And why should I settle on Kateri when so many others are part of the earth on which we stand? Names long gone, villages rubbed clear off the map, centuries of stories, stores of memory—of certain springtime rains and advice on how to best handle a mother-in-law. Gone now, those called *Snow Woman*, *Laughing Girl*, and *Daughter of the Meadow*. Gone now, queen and saint and storyteller alike. How I wish I could go back to 1884 and free Zitkala-Ša from that chair, help the child find her way over the plains and back to her mother. It's too much to hope that such a girl might make an escape, but logic has no foothold in the realm of desire, and it's the wildness I want. I want to be brave enough to untie that girl, saving her braids for her, but also for me, and for all of us perhaps, which is why, finally, I will write about The Other Magpie.

6. The Other Magpie painted her face yellow and fixed a stuffed woodpecker in her hair like a warrior might do. A pretty woman, she could have had a man but remained single in her midtwenties. 1876. The year of the American Centennial. The year of the Battle of the Rosebud in Montana Territory. Two hundred years after Kateri fled to New France and remade herself in the image of a saint, eight years before the cutting of Zitkala-Ša's hair, one hundred thirty-five years before a fawn tried its legs at a stream near a marsh where beads dangled from a nearby branch, The Other Magpie pushed a knife into her belt, unleashed a war song, and rode her horse straight into the face of the enemy.

7. Government troops had already encroached across the plains, pushing into territory promised to the Sioux a few years before. But when the Black Hills were discovered to have gold, promises evaporated, and U.S. troops once again took up arms. Enemies of the Sioux, the Crow were easily recruited as government allies in the Great Sioux War of 1876.

Crow women occasionally accompanied men as they prepared for battle. What was unusual was The Other Magpie's participation in the battle itself. Unusual, but not impossible. The Other Magpie would have heard stories of Pine Leaf, the woman who'd counted coup nearly fifty years before—a woman who became both warrior and chief. Pine Leaf wore a dress decorated with beads and elk teeth like other Crow women, but she took several wives of her own. And while The Other Magpie would not have known it, Calamity Jane was said to ride among the U.S. forces, disguised as a man. Another woman, a Cheyenne called Buffalo Calf Road Woman, not only saved her brother at Rosebud but was said to deliver the strike that threw Custer from his horse at the battle at Little Big Horn ten days later.

But such stories only emerged after the battle. As The Other Magpie advanced north toward Rosebud Creek, she had only the vengeance she'd promised after her brother was killed by Crazy Horse and the Lakota Sioux.

8. Armed with only her belt knife while the men carried rifles, The Other Magpie rode beside Finds-Them-And-Kills-Them, a man whose hair hung in braids in the style of a woman. Finds-Them was born into the body of a male but was, in most things, a woman—such people were considered *badé* (two-spirits) by the Crow, who allowed for such ambiguity. What a sight they must have made as they rode into battle, a warrior dressed as a woman beside a woman as wild as any man.

When they came under attack by the Sioux, the duo was fierce, leaping into a battle that stretched miles and lasted for six bloody hours. When Finds-Them attempted to aid a fallen Crow, shooting at an approaching Lakota to save him, The Other Magpie charged at the Sioux warrior with nothing but her holler and coup stick, the red plumage of a bird blazing in her hair. The sound and the sight sent men in the other direction, allowing her to approach and count coup against the Lakota warrior—scoring honor points for touching him with her willow stick. Whether she killed the enemy with her own knife or he was stopped by the shot from Finds-Them's rifle, it was The Other Magpie who swooped in for the scalp, one of eleven taken by the Crow that day.

The U.S. forces claimed victory when the Sioux finally fell back, but the government troops were exhausted, and it was their allies, the

Crow, who'd held the line and sang their way back to camp. The Other Magpie howled along with the men, face painted yellow, necklaces rattling as her black horse leaped over creek bed and fallen tree, pausing only to tie a feather to the end of her coup stick for all the world to see.

9. The magpie is a handsome bird: black and white, with wings and long tail feathers—when caught in the light, its feathers show iridescent. Found primarily west of the Rockies, the American magpie is a member of the same family as crows and ravens. They are intelligent birds—one of the few animals to recognize itself in a mirror. Magpies are known to hold "funerals"—one bird calling out when another is found dead, cawing to other birds, who fly in and surround the body with their raucous song. They're also accomplished hoarders, collecting food and bits of string and metal, which they stash in caches to return to later. But even more than their intelligence, the magpies' daring is a necessary trait in the stark western landscape.

Before the Plains Indians were removed and the buffalo slaughtered, magpies followed their movement, for both bird and tribe relied on herds of bison to sustain them. After the arrival of Europeans, the magpie had no choice but to adapt, surviving by learning to steal eggs, landing on the backs of cows to scavenge ticks, descending on carrion, swaggering as they stroll roadsides, picking over accidents, making feasts of someone else's kill.

10. Which brings me back to the fake Indian, a woman who covers her fingers in turquoise, who wears a buckskin dress and makes nature paintings and goes to schools to tell children of the Cayuga, the Cherokee, the Cree. She calls herself Leona Moon-Heron and dyes her blonde hair black and sets it under a beaded headband. Her clothing is a mash of traditions, southwestern vests paired with eastern moccasins. She looks like someone playing a part, with her turquoise and headband, like an actress in a small-town play.

11. Is it possible that most people have little concept of what an Indian looks like? They are here and not here, hidden on reservations and sometimes settling into nearby cities. Is it possible that we do not see them? And if so, where's the harm in someone claiming to be Native and going to schools to tell stories about the coming of winter and the storing of corn, speaking with reverence of our sister the squash while making paintings of the white dog and the longhouse? Aren't we all looking for something to connect us to others while locating the truth of who we are? If you want to be Sioux, perhaps you are. Maybe Leona is of two spirits in this regard, caught between desire and reality, and why should anyone be limited by the story she happens to be born into? It's petty, I think, to worry whether someone is or is not what she claims to be—petty and overreaching and perhaps even cruel, yet I find I cannot let it go.

12. I went to a funeral on the reservation last summer. A young man in a ribboned shirt and feathered cap chanted over the body; a single feather jutting from his headdress in the manner of the Seneca. I listened to the language and watched those around me, their dark eyes turning inward, remembering the elder who'd so recently stood among them. Could they see by the blue of my eye that I was not of them, though I sat with them? Of course. I'd lived on the reservation only briefly, but long enough to know that pale skin does not go unnoticed. And more telling than the color of my eye was its direction, which traveled the length of the longhouse—the whole of my body taking in the scent of smoke, the creak of communal bench, the sound of the old language turning like pebble and turkey feather in the throat. No matter what blood I might carry, the real difference was my eye. The way it turned outward and took.

13. Leona Moon-Heron is probably, in part, a real Indian. There's likely a grandparent with Native blood, a great-grandparent who once lived on a reservation. Perhaps she's like another of my sisters, one of four girls without an Iroquois father who'd calculated our percentage based on a grandmother reported to be Mohawk. After scribbling out the math, she declared us almost a sixth. 'Almost a Sixth,' I called her for years, mocking her desire to stake and lay claim, but then, nearly every poor person we ever knew claimed Native blood, and our own family heritage is so messy it's nearly impossible to sort through the

strands. I mocked my sister, but I too craved the warm coat of identity. Especially one so appealing, tied as it is to nature. But how to square it with history and reservation realities, not nearly so romantic?

My baby sister, part Iroquois—I realize now why I see her as that fawn, she who is grown but seems always on shaky ground, she who is beautiful but often shivers. A tender thing, to be a fawn. It will break the hearts of those who watch it struggle to its feet. But what does this have to do with Leona and what it means to be Native, and why I should care if anyone claims an identity that isn't even mine?

The information she shares, while filtered and perfumed, is probably correct. Her heart, I'm almost certain, is good. And isn't it better for third-graders to get a visit from a faux Native for their unit on local history than no Native at all?

¶4. No. The answer has to be no. Because of saints marked by smallpox, lost queens, and villages burned to the ground. Because of battles waged along rivers, land taken and given and taken again. The answer must be no. Because of shivering sisters and houses without plumbing on swaths of land on which most of us never tread. I must object because Leona is too pretty a package, by which I do not mean her features so much as the ugliness that her paintings and school visits hide. The scarcity of real Indians is its own lesson. The fact that the traces of those who once lived here are most evident in the names of schools and shopping malls is truth, and the truth means something. It must. The genuine article—though harder to come by and more difficult to digest—may be as close to wildness as we get.

¶5. *A wild band of Indians.* Once considered an insult, human wildness is a precious and fleeting thing. Wildness. Living in a state of nature. It's what we admire in children, their precocious honesty, grounded by belly laughs and full-hearted sobs. It's what we admire so much, then promptly eradicate. If we're lucky or wealthy at middle age, those of us who tend toward personal growth might attempt to recover our "true" selves through hypnosis, pilgrimages in northern Spain, or retreats in the monasteries of Tibet, doing our best to find our way back to something buried under the rubble of storage units, five kinds of forks, and packets of artificial sweetener. So cluttered are our paths, who can be blamed for taking up a tradition that is not her own, a tradition tied to a past, that seems closer, truer, wilder somehow?

I understand but resist and return to the image of a child in a chair, held by straps and hands and whatever it takes to keep her still.

A child, the moment before her hair is cut. Face wet, eyes bulging, struggling to flee from those who want to tame her. How much easier to relate to her, the innocent about to be severed in ways we still can't fathom. How much more difficult to see ourselves in the one who binds and cuts. But there's something to looking at the white hand straight on, isn't there? Something necessary about holding the scissors in our gaze long enough to recognize the reflection showing in the blade. Something true about the blue eye and what is has sometimes meant.

Valaida Snow took to the stage at a time when female instrumental-ists were notably absent from the burgeoning jazz scene, but like other African American performers, Valaida found more appreciative audi-ences in Europe and Asia than at home.

FREEZE-FRAME

Paris, 1939. A nightclub scene. Just a two-minute clip of a film starring Maurice Chevalier and Marie Deá. The singer in a shimmy dress should hardly stand out—an American jazz singer in Paris, she's intended to be atmospheric as the smoke rising in slow turns from the cigarette in the lead actress's hand. The scene is a jumble of intrigue; jaunty leading lady and flash of French teeth, but Valaida is all I really see. Holding a trumpet, with her big smile and golden skin. A woman who'd pushed her way up from east Tennessee, working her way through the speakeasies of Harlem to the nightclubs of Paris, to arrive at this reel of film, where, even after all these years, though the scene has crumbled—the actors and their highball glasses have crumbled and even Valaida herself is long gone—I can hit *play* and set her loose, voice and horn unwinding into song, her sound and shine lodged forever on a strip of celluloid.

The individual images that make up a film are called *frames*. During projection, a rotating shutter creates flashes of darkness between them. A phenomenon known as *persistence of vision* keeps viewers from noticing these spaces, and the image lingers in the human eye even after the source is removed, forming bridges from one image to the next, creating the perception of motion.

In the early days of movies, sequences came sixteen frames per second, which lent the motion a jittery quality. Sound was added and technology improved, film sequences increased to twenty-four frames per second, making the movement smooth and lifelike. Which is how Valaida appears in the clip, a woman in perpetual motion, coming at us at twenty-four frames per beat.

Pièges, the movie is called. French for *trap*, the word refers to pitfalls, entanglements, and snares. But whether it's set in English or French, a good trap comes down to something wanted and something caught, the scrape of a lock sliding into place before one realizes she has stepped into a cage. A clamp coming down upon the animal's foot, the hook finding the tender part of the fish. The most dangerous traps are constructed not of metal but words. The offer of another drink, *just one more*, the promise of a new job, easy money, the breadcrumb trail, twigs and twine, the tripped wire, the pull of temptation, *must you really go?* the bigger house, the marriage proposal, cures for boredom, *no one needs to know*, the open wound of regret and sticky hands of the past, one last peek over the shoulder.

1939. For a black woman from the American South, a French film may not be such a bad place to be trapped. Everything is black and white, but the director makes full use of shadow and light, the camera blurring a circle of brass, big as the moon, before pulling back to reveal the flare of trumpet, finger waves, a man at the piano tapping his foot, and a woman in the sparkling dress: *Sweetheart, there's heaven in your eyes . . .*

Freeze-frame: the moment in a film when all action seems to stop. By inserting a series of duplicate images into a sequence of frames, the moment is suspended, and we experience the sensation of an image caught and held.

But the stillness is only an illusion. What appears unmoving is alive with the whir of reel and electricity, so that the frozen image, so solid in its stillness, is, in fact, a tangle of movement and light.

There's murder at work in the film, a killer using classifieds to lure and prey on unsuspecting women. He's all hook, and they're all fish. But there's something else, a plot to catch the man, a trap making use of the lovely Marie Deá, so that the tables are turned. The woman becomes a hook and the killer a fish. Valaida is part of the backdrop, along with the piano and a potted plant. No, she's not part of the scripted action of the film, but surely she must sense it, as she opens her mouth to sing the song—the thrum of the trap tightening, the shift in the air, the million ways to be caught.

Little Louis they called her—*Louis*, for the way she played like Satchmo. *Little* because even with such big talent, she was still a woman.

Queen of the Horn, they said. Because—more than the singing and dancing and smiling in a way that lassoed the sun onto whatever stage she occupied—the trumpet was her gift and the way she stood before the crowd, all vibration and flutter, growling into that brass.

Queen of the Trumpet, some said. But I think of her as Lady Valaida; *Lady* for the fineness implied and for the sound—the long *a* snuggling up against the notes of her first name, like a song when you say it: *Lady Valaida.*

Europe is a haven, a heaven, until the war. A year after her nightclub scene in *Pièges*, the backdrop begins to change. Even the film's director, the German-born Siodmak, knows enough to leave, taking the last ship out of France on the eve of German occupation. But for him, leaving is a new beginning. He will make a home in America and the best-known films of his career there. Not so Valaida. If she has a home, it's a moving ship, or the seat in the back of a taxi, or perhaps the center of a lighted stage.

Friends caution her against staying, warning of German intent, pointing to mounting evidence of the dark storms brewing. But Valaida's been floating around Europe for years; what else does she know? She flashes her dimples, making light of Nazi talk. She's had her share of troubles, alcohol and men, morphine and boys, sources of pleasure turned to pain. Yes, Valaida knows a thing or two about traps, but even she will be surprised when the Germans push into Denmark and soldiers pluck her from the stage, replacing the song in her mouth with the sound of prison doors closing behind her.

.✦.

Some say two years, others say not quite so long. In some accounts, the prison is a German holding center, in others, a Danish jail. Valaida herself said it was a concentration camp. Either way, she was held captive by the Nazis during the war.

She'd come up in 1920s America, a time when women didn't play horns and blacks weren't invited onto stages with whites. Not easily. Not regularly. Even later—in the thirties and forties, once jazz had pushed beyond the South and become America's sound, things loosened some, and white bands played with blacks—even then the musicians were usually men. The girl who'd made her way from the Jim Crow South, fought her way onto the stage in 1920s America, even that girl, with all her pluck and fire, would be hard-pressed not to be broken after being held in one place for the first time in her adult life.

.✦.

Good God, what they would do with her today.

Magazine covers, talk shows, and tell-alls, celebrities vying to play Valaida in the biopic. Who in her right mind wouldn't want to wrap herself in a silk gown and push an orchid behind her ear? Who would not want to fold herself into the warm hum of audience and stage light? All New York would buzz over those dresses, the fluff and pull of the boas she insists upon—everyone hazarding guesses about which man she's stepping out with tonight. All of this before she even opens her mouth, before she lifts that horn and blows us all away.

.✦.

It's possible, of course, that she'd slip once again through the cracks. Even a century later, Valaida might still pack her trunks and leave for Paris, making stage of castles and courtyards, counting royalty among her fans. Perhaps the pattern would be repeated, the years of roving across the sea, the back and forth: New York and London, New York and Rome, New York and Moscow. Even Asia. How they adored Valaida. How they smiled and issued invitations and served her up like the finest dish.

It's possible there'd still be the morphine, the boys, and the final collapse at the Palace Theater at the age of fifty-two. Even today. Especially today.

But for all the clamor, for all the ships to Tokyo, Jakarta, and Shanghai, for all the elegant dresses and orchids delivered fresh to her dressing-room door, for all her strut and sashay and hot trumpet playing—the world settled quickly around the spaces Valaida vacated, beginning to take up the air she breathed before she even finished her last exhale.

She's caught forever in my imagination as a young woman just arrived from Chattanooga. On the streets of Harlem, with a wide smile and spit curls, instrument in hand. There she is on Broadway, at the film studio, headlining at the Apollo, singing and dancing, taking as much of America by storm as color and gender allow, playing and singing, life coming at her hard and fast.

How her voice has not been remembered is its own wonder. Constricted by the times into coquettish ribbons, the vocals are high and tight—but now and then something comes through, low notes, something of the horn embedded into Valaida's voice, the insistence of it, the brass, blue and swollen, ripping the words apart at their seams.

Perhaps it was the making of sound, then, that was most like home, Valaida emptying her breath into her instrument the way her mother had taught her brother and two sisters—their mother taught them to play cello and bass, accordion and saxophone. But it was the slick bend of yellow metal that grabbed little Valaida, the trumpet whose call sounded most familiar. She picked up that horn, tiny girl, and began to make herself a terrific noise.

Did she play the White Elephant Saloon with her sisters like Bessie Smith before her? There are stories of an early marriage, her girlhood cut short. But what was life before then, before the men and movement and the day she played background in a French film? What did she think when she looked into the Tennessee River? Toward Lookout Mountain rising from the south—what sounds did the world whisper to little black girls in 1903?

Jazz is restless, the trombonist J. J. Johnson once said. *It won't stay put.*

The clip of French film is only two minutes, but two minutes can contain entire worlds. All those frames per second, the air turning with plumes of smoke and desire, the lush jumble of French words, the actress with her lustrous eyes tamping out a new cigarette and the man with the newspaper folded in half, a photograph stashed inside—the murderer perhaps—but now Valaida has started singing again: *I loved you from the start.*

She takes up her trumpet as the camera cuts away to the actress slipping into a chair, talking with such ease she cannot help but tempt the eye, the sweet mash of martini and conversation. But even she is no match for the pull of Valaida's voice, which saturates the scene, obscuring the leading lady with her perfect pout, the man and his newspaper, until the words become a distraction from the music, the actors and the plot become background to the sound of breath coming clean through the brass: the jubilant blare, loud and bright, but tender, too, in places.

Paris, 1939. The clink of glasses and the scent of roses rises from the inside of women's wrists. But nothing is more alive than Valaida and the way she makes that trumpet sing.

Memory is a goddess draped in silk in a painting by Rossetti, the name on a headstone in a Memphis cemetery, and the word we use to describe impressions that rise up from the past, those images and sounds that serve as both remedy to and result of the passing of time.

A GIRL CALLED MEMORY
A TRIPTYCH

1. A girl called Memory, I swear she was there. Beneath the earth at Elmwood Cemetery, a few feet from the one called Magnolia, surrounded by Evalines and Lucindas and more Eula Maes than you can count. Her name, carved large across the top of the stone. Memory. It stopped me, that name. Unexpected as the woman named *Submit* in a pioneer cemetery in Vermont. Dead at thirty, Submit's stone said, and I thought how fitting some names. Submit. Lying in a township called Eden, the Lamoille River Valley opening before her. I will not soon forget Submit. Even now, I know just where she rests. But what has become of Memory? I have walked among southern trees, enjoying their tremendous bloom in spring, trampling their scarlet seeds in fall. I have walked upon the Confederate dead, tread the bones of those lost to yellow fever, contemplated the lives of heroes and spies and hookers with hearts of gold, but still and all, I cannot find her. A girl called Memory. I swear, I swear, I once saw her there.

2. A girl called Memory. *Mnemosyne.* Goddess of language. Patroness of words. In a painting by Rossetti, Memory holds a lamp, but the smooth expanse of flesh is what lends the canvas its light. Sweet-talked by Zeus, they say, Memory stretched out with him for nine nights and gave birth, in turn, to the nine Muses. One wonders about those nights, Zeus's touch, warm with practice, all that hair, the flickering lamp, her

way with words, his appetite. Mother of Poetry, Music, and Dance. Astronomy is Memory's child, even Comedy feeds at her breast. What nights they must have been. The way she would have replayed them by the yellow glow of her lamp. Nine nights soaked like figs in brandy. Nine nights made headier with each backward glance—his hands, her mouth, the way morning light finally came as it did, filtered through the branches.

5. A girl called Memory, and Memory tilted her lamp to illuminate a moment from forty years before. Swish of auburn hair as a mother bends into her child, playing with its toes. *This little piggy went to market, this little piggy stayed home, this little piggy had roast beef* . . . . "But which pig had none!" I'd squeal, knowing it was the fourth but wanting to hear the rhyme once more, wanting her to once again play the pigs on my toes, keys to a piano, the music, until finally, the last toe—*wee wee wee all the way home*—the tickle of skin, the laughter, hers and mine, coming like cathedral bells, the joyful rolling sound. So many children, but in this moment, it's just us, all pigs and laughter and toes.

A simple thing, memory. But enough to stop a grown woman from washing dishes. Enough to make her find the nearest chair to fall into when such moments descend, leaving her no choice but to bring her hands to her face. How close it is: the singsong voice, the tender flesh, pure delight . . . and something else, something unfolding from deeper still, something I once knew. *All the way, all the way home.*

Time cannot break the bird's wing from the bird.

—EDNA ST. VINCENT MILLAY

RETURN TO
THE DREAMLAND

Sunset, and Susan B. steps from the trolley to the lakeshore.

"Charlotte?" she asks, and I nod.

Even in her day, the place where the mouth of the Genesee opens to Lake Ontario was called Charlotte. Our lives are separated by more than a century, but time is flimsy tonight and we stand together at the headlands, the shoreline split by Irondequoit Bay, with beaches on both sides, ladies in white dresses strolling boardwalks, hotels with verandas, concession stands and gardens, the screech of gulls as the sky goes from blue to pink, and families pack up for the day.

"Hurry," I say to Susan, who's unsteady from so much time off her feet. She isn't used to taking orders but is so astounded to find herself once again breathing that she follows like a child.

"The carousel—installed just before I fell sick." Her voice is slow, words measured, even as her hand flies to her heart as if checking to be sure it's still inside her chest.

"Come," I say and push toward the soft glow of lights. The sound of cymbals fills the air as if a circus band has made its way into the pavilion, and it's only as we step onto the platform that Susan notices her shoes—cream silk T-straps, fine Cuban heels.

"What's this?" she asks as she takes in the stretch of exposed leg. She bends and runs a finger over the hose, feeling for the first time the miracle of rayon, then notices the cut of her dress and becomes so mesmerized by the glint of beads that she's in danger of falling under a permanent spell—but she straightens herself and catches my arm.

"See here," she says, but I point to others—women swishing past in drop-waist dresses, hemlines barely touching their knees as they choose from the menagerie of animals mounted on poles and make seats of tiger and ostrich. Susan pushes a hand through her hair and slowly understands that it's gone, the bun over her ears. Cut to the chin, her dark strands have gone curly in the late summer heat.

She's silent as she sets a hand on the rump of a wooden horse. The music from the organ is tinny and sweet, broken by the sound of the ticket man saying *Everyone please find a seat*.

"Come on, Susan," I shout. "You can have a horse any old time." I point to an oversized pig and a cat holding a fish between its teeth, and poor old Susan, she must still be in shock for how easily she complies. And when the machine starts up, it's like being inside a music box, Susan B. perched on her fish-eating cat and me on my pig with its snout raised, hooves high in the air. A circle of animals rises and falls to the music, lulling us as the beach and sky flash by, the blues so swollen all points of division blur, the air scented with peanuts and candy apples. Susan's grip loosens on the pole and her face goes soft in the last bit of light.

The moment is broken by a pack of girls, louder than gulls, seven or eight young women, arms linked, a chorus of laughter and the intermittent squawk of their party horns. Gone are the corsets, gone the petticoats; the girls in their baggy dresses could be boys except for their arms, which are bare and ornamented with bangles and falls of beadwork and fringe. Their stockings are rolled low, exposing powdered knees as they blow kisses to the whole of the carousel—what can Susan make of such women, so rough and so pretty?

They hop the gate and rush the platform, the man in the red-striped shirt shouting, "Ladies, ladies—come now, you'll just have to wait!"

They laugh, as if they have never once considered the word *wait* and teeter along the wooden planks, balancing on the moving floor. One lands directly in front of us, a girl whose dress is the same pinkish color as her flesh so that she looks nude on her horse, a glittery Godiva, tucking bobbed strands behind her ear, turning to wink before lifting her party horn into the air.

"A celebration?" Susan can't peel her eyes from the girl—though it's tough to say whether the suffragist is transfixed by the dress or the girl's manner, both of which are exuberant and loose.

"It's 1920," I shout. "August the twenty-sixth."

Susan B. looks inward, trying to make sense of time. March when she died, all the trees on Madison Street still empty of leaves. I watch her work out the math. Fourteen years since 1906.

"Your amendment was adopted today," I say, "The Nineteenth—the one you drafted back in 1878."

Suddenly all grogginess is gone. Susan turns sidesaddle on her cat and leans in. "But what were the others? The amendments? The Sixteenth, Seventeenth, and the Eighteenth?"

"Let's leave that a minute," I say. "Women will vote for president in a few months." I touch her hand. "All your work has finally come to pass."

Not even a flicker of pride shows in her face, which remains cool in the stream of movement and light. Godiva hangs from her horse like a trick rider, but Susan's no longer paying attention. When she speaks again, her voice is so quiet I must strain to hear.

"But where are the others? Elizabeth Stanton? Anna Shaw? My sister Mary?"

She turns around, eyes working to take it all in, looking for a split second as if she might come undone. But Susan B. is nothing if not backbone, and she holds it together, settling again onto her carved wooden cat, watching as strange faces circle past.

Just like that, we're on the other side of the bay, in the dance hall built over a ravine—the Dreamland. It will burn in 1923, but that's three years away, and how elegant she looks tonight, Miss Susan, dark waves smoothed and oiled, drop earrings flattering her neckline, a single silver bangle pushed halfway up her arm. If you didn't know better, you might call her Goddess of the Dance Hall. If you only noticed the hair, the low-cut dress, and the way she stands, hands on hips, you'd think her a bit of a catch—a scamp, perhaps, with those red-painted lips. If she's uncomfortable—this woman most often seen in fussy black gowns that lend her the air of a widow or schoolmarm—she doesn't show it, standing in a dress the color of candlelight, perfume set into the hollow of her neck.

The hall is packed. Couples glide out on the dance floor; some move into shadowy corners. Two large men unload bottles from a box and stack them under a table, a hushed urgency to their work. Before Susan can ask what's going on, the women from the carousel appear, a flock of boozy angels. They perch on the table, jaunty and sly—whether hiding the liquor or ornamenting the makeshift bar, it's hard to say. They've smudged their eyes with kohl and made their brows into skinny lines so that in the low light, they look like a row of Kewpie dolls.

"You'd be astounded by the business of makeup," I say a tad too fast, trying to avoid the subject of Prohibition, and as if on cue, the Kewpies remove tubes from their clutches and remake the bowties of their lips. *Is this the freedom you meant?* I want to ask as we watch them work but instead only say, "What a night."

"What a night," I repeat when Susan doesn't answer, and it's true. The air is fine up near the lake, cooling the skin, every last breeze feeling as if it was made just for us.

"Why have you brought me here?" Susan B. turns suddenly, blue eyes flashing. "What is this—something like in the story by Dickens?"

"Sort of," I say. "Only you're the ghost."

When I hear how harsh the words sound, I whisper, "They teach us about you in school, you know."

She looks surprised, this woman who spent her life traveling over hard roads, thousands of miles, crisscrossing the country to speak, withstanding public ridicule and assaults of rotten fruit and ugly words for voicing her belief that women should be counted.

"What do they say about me?" The voice is stern, but with her new hair, she looks like Louise Brooks as I tell her about the insistence on equality, her determination and hard work, leaving out the fact that the lessons are not lively, that I myself did not much care for her hard-faced silhouette—is this a penance then, I wonder, for all those years as a schoolgirl when I could not quite bring myself to like her? But no. As we stand together, there's something else, a sort of affection for this woman pulled from time and gazing about, trying to make sense of so much strangeness. Just a handful of years, but the world does not stay still, and it's a new place.

"I only wanted to stand with you for a time," I say, "and this is a day I thought you might like to see."

Now she's firing off questions. *Who is president? How has the local university done in their admission of women? What about women's pay—does it now finally equal men's?*

I open my mouth to reply, but she's suddenly too close, and the scent of her perfume combined with the press of her questions is too much. What should I report? The Great War, the new prosperity, automobiles in every driveway, women in pants—the way Coco Chanel finally accomplished with haute couture what Amelia Bloomer started seventy years prior, the way the New Woman looks strangely like an adolescent girl or a dapper young man. How it's progress and not progress at once, women's pay not equal to men's in 1920, nor nearly a century later. I could try for regional pride, telling how New York granted women the vote three years ago—1917—but the truth is that our very own county voted it down. *Thank god for Buffalo*, I might say, to lighten the mood. Or talk poetry. Recite lines by H.D. (*I should have thought / in a dream you would have brought / some lovely, perilous thing*) or Langston Hughes (*What happens to a dream deferred?*). Should I tell her about jazz and dance, plays by Eugene O'Neill, the new American voices, bubbling under the surface for so long, now rising in ways that can't be turned back.

She waits, leaning in, but I cannot answer and stay silent, watching the women with their slack dresses and short hair, free and not free, on this late August night.

"After all those years, we're finally to be counted," Susan says. No longer pressing for answers, she lets the reality of the Nineteenth Amendment sink in as the moon rises higher in the sky. "All those years," she repeats, something catching in her throat.

I set my hand on her shoulder and let it rest.

"Here," I say, after too much silence has passed. "Have a sip of this." But Susan only stiffens and turns up a painted lip. We stand, a few long moments, me enjoying the rub of whiskey, Susan so quiet at my side I think she might be weeping.

"Come now," I say, pushing the glass in her direction. "It's a celebration."

She turns on me, eyes gone hawkish so that even in her beaded dress she becomes the face chiseled into the silver dollar, the coin America never took to. But I keep to myself talk of the Susan B. dollar and the reality of low voter turnout.

"Time for some fresh air." I take her elbow and steer us toward the door, where a musician on break steps aside to let us pass.

"Wait for us!" The Kewpies follow with a bottle of champagne, and it seems they've recognized Susan B. and one of the girls grabs her hand.

"Here, here to our Susan," another voice calls—and do I catch something of a smile from Miss Anthony at the word "our," a softening in her eyes as young people begin to gather around, a chorus of voices saying, "Hurrah" and "Cheers," while lifting high their glasses?

Over the lake, fireworks.

"Would you look at that," the crowd whispers as they gather in the field next door, everyone, even the orchestra with their instruments, oohing and ahhing and rushing out. Tiny doilies of Queen Anne's lace brush against our legs as we move, fireworks exploding overhead.

Susan's face is lit with a smile as the lights sizzle over the lake.

"Don't you like the display?" she asks, wondering at my quiet.

I nod, looking at Susan in her finery. She cuts a lovelier figure, yes, but I realize now that something of the old style became her.

"I'm sorry," I say. "Sorry about the hair, the makeup, and the clothes."

She only breathes deeply the night air. Something has gotten into her, a bit of the fireworks, the sound of jazz. She looks around at the sight of so many women, all of them looking skyward.

"There's nothing wrong with some time among the stars," she says.

"Yes." I nod and spy two girls, the younger in dark braids, leaning in and whispering in the manner of sisters as they stand before us.

"Look there," I whisper. "I believe those are the Fox sisters."

When she doesn't respond, I turn and see that Susan is no longer beside me. A few steps off, she's found her sister Mary, and they're caught in an embrace. Another girl approaches, dark eyes and pale skin, a handsome woman at her side, the pair call out greetings to the Anthonys as if they are old friends. May and Celestia. I turn and spy a woman emerging from the woods in a scarlet skirt, her figure shining so brightly she looks to have fallen from the fireworks display.

"La Spelterina," I say with a gasp. She nods as she passes on her way toward the cliffs, followed by two young women speaking in hushed Memphis voices. Alice and Freda, holding hands as they delight in Maria's costume and her standing so close to the edge. A woman floats by in a silk gown, trumpet in one hand, the other leading a child who carries the scent of sea on her skin.

They keep coming. A woman near the hall ties up her horse, and shows one of the bootleggers the willow stick she carries, a cluster of feathers tied to its end. A trio of girls follow in her wake, girls in 1970s fashions I know; I run to them as others arrive. Women and girls slipping into the meadow the way one slips into the undertow of a dream.

The time between darkness and waking. The twilight hour. That's where we are. Voices everywhere. The sound of Irish breaking like water over old stones, a Louisiana patois, and the sound of the orchestra starting a new song, with Valaida at the helm. Such a sweet song, and everyone turning together for a moment in the field. Beside me now, a woman with a face I've seen before but can't quite place—and as if conjured by her beauty, a man with a camera.

"Stand tall, ladies." he says. "Let's have a portrait for posterity."

And it must be the word *posterity* that sets us off, or else the word *ladies*, which seems all wrong out in the field, where girls in short dresses laugh and tumble into tall grasses, drowsy and giddy at once.

For posterity! Someone repeats—there must be thousands of us now —huddling together as the camera is set up. More women than you can imagine, standing side by side as the photographer fidgets with his settings.

"Best to make that lens wide," comes a booming voice, and we know it's Mabel by the way Ontario erupts into waves. We laugh again, but, of course, she's right. So many of us. The big and the small, the plain and the spangled, the fierce and the timid and those occupying the spaces in between. All of us together. Best to make that lens wide.

ACKNOWLEDGMENTS

With grateful acknowledgement to the editors and journals in which earlier versions of these essays appeared:

"Sly Foxes"	*Bellingham Review* (2015)
"We Ghosts"	*The McNeese Review* (2015)
"A Thousand Mary Doyles"	*Short Takes: Brief Encounters with Contemporary Fiction* (New York: W. W. Norton, 2005)
	Brevity (2014)
"Mad Love"	*Southern Sin: True Stories of the Sultry South and Women Behaving Badly* (Pittsburg: In Fact Books, 2014)
	Creative Nonfiction (2013)
"Dare"	*Waccamaw* (2011)
"Twyla"	*You: An Anthology of Essays Devoted to the Second Person* (Gettysburg, Pa.: Welcome Table Press, 2013)
"Human Curiosity"	*South Loop Review* (2013)
"Rosalie, from the Philippines"	*Louisville Review* (2014)
"Blue Kentucky Girl"	*Appalachian Heritage Magazine* (2014)
"Freeze-Frame"	*Zone 3* (2015)
"A Girl Called Memory"	*Twelfth House* (2014)

MANY THANKS

To Lisa Bayer, John Griswold, Rebecca Norton, Kaelin Chappell Broaddus, Barbara Wojhoski, and the University of Georgia Press for their stewardship of this project and the fine books they usher into the world. To Judith Kitchen, for her example. To Dinty W. Moore, Jason Howard, Amy Wright, Brenda Miller, Dinah Lenney, Rachel Wilkinson, and Joe Oestreich for their placement of my work. To Lee Martin, Kristen Iversen, Harriet Scott Chessman, Jim Mott, Gregory Gerard, James Graves, Jenny Lloyd, Lee McAvoy, Elizabeth Osta, Sally Parker, Maureen McGuire, and Devon Taylor for their careful readings. To my colleagues at the University of Memphis and my students in Memphis, West Virginia, Rochester, and beyond. To Mount Hope Cemetery and the Susan B. Anthony House in Rochester and the Elmwood Cemetery in Memphis for the programs they provide to keep alive legacies that might otherwise be forgotten. To my friends and family (Livingstons, Motts, Heywoods, Skyes, Rosarios, Goforths, Wilson). To my mother and her mother and the women before and after who lived outside the lines.

SOURCES

EPIGRAPHS

The epigraph is taken from *Half in Shade: Family, Photography, and Fate*, by Judith Kitchen (Minneapolis: Coffee House Press, 2012).

Sly Foxes

"My Little Grass Shack in Kealakekua, Hawaii," written by Bill Cogswell, Tommy Harrison, and Johnny Noble (New York: Miller Music, 1933). Only the title is used.

We Ghosts

The epigraph is taken from *Nightwood*, by Djuna Barnes (London: Faber & Faber, 1936).

Some Names and What They Mean

The epigraph appears in *The Rutledge Book of World Proverbs*, by John R. Stone (New York: Routledge, 2006).

Some details about the Alphabet Murder victims and the crimes in Rochester, New York, are taken from *Alphabet Killer: The True Story of the Double Initial Murders*, by Cheri Farnsworth (Mechanicsburg, Pa.: Stackpole Books, 2010).

Mad Love: The Ballad of Fred & Allie

Information about the murder and trials, including letters between Alice and Freda, is taken from *Sapphic Slashers: Sex, Violence, and American Modernity*, by Lisa Duggan (Durham, N.C.: Duke University Press, 2000).

Articles and other sources are cited in the text.

Dare

Information on the Roanoke voyage comes from the *The fourth Voyage made to Virginia with three ships, in the yere 1587. Wherein was transported the second Colonie*, by Richard Hakluyt (Glasgow: James MacLehose and Sons, 1587). Available online through the University of Virginia at http://jefferson.village .virginia.edu/vcdh/jamestown.

The Goddess of Ogdensburg:
A Rise and Fall in Seventeen Poses

Information on Audrey comes from the thorough work in *Queen of the Artists' Studios*, by Andrea Geyer (New York: Art in General, 2007) and a series of articles by Audrey Munson for the *New York American* in 1921.

The epigraph is taken from an article that appeared in the *American Weekly Sunday Supplement* to the *New York American* in 1921, quoted in the Geyer volume.

Information is also taken from the following *New York Times* articles:

"Audrey Munson Takes Dose of Poison: Artists' Model's in Critical Condition at Her Northern New York Birthplace," May 28, 1922.

"Audrey Munson Is Out of Danger; Model Who Attempted Suicide by Poison Will Recover, Her Physician Says. PENITENT, WANTS TO LIVE, Says Powerful Influences Persecute Her—Silent about a Telegram Believed from Fiance," May 29, 1922.

"Seek Wilkins Witness; Ticket Taker Saw Murdered Woman Alone in Station," March 25, 1919.

Big

The epigraph is taken from the poem "Käthe Kollwitz," from *The Speed of Darkness*, by Muriel Rukeyser (New York: Random House, 1968).

Visuals and inspiration come from the documentary *Jazz on a Summer's Day*, by Bert Stern and Aram Avakian (New Yorker Films, 1960). No lyrics are used.

Manuela, with a Hip

The lines of Shakespeare come from *The Merchant of Venice*.

The lines of Millay are taken from "What lips my lips have kissed, and where, and why / Sonnet XLIII," by Edna St. Vincent Millay, in *Collected Poems*, (New York: Harper & Row, 1956).

On Seeing Weather-Beaten Trees:
A Study in Two Photographs

The epigraph comes from the poem "Adelaide Crapsey," by Carl Sandburg, in *Cornhuskers* (New York: Henry Holt, 1918).

The poems "On Seeing Weather-Beaten Trees" and "Amaze," by Adelaide Crapsey are taken from *Verse*, published posthumously by Claude Bragdon (New York: Manas Press, 1915).

Colton Johnson, Vassar College historian, provided helpful information on Adelaide's time at Vassar and the first photograph, shown in the Vassar Encyclopedia (online).

The second photo referred to in the essay, titled "Adelaide of Saranac," can be found on the website of writer Karen Alkalay-Gut, author of *Alone in the Dawn: The Life of Adelaide Crapsey* (Athens: University of Georgia Press, 1988).

Heroines of the Ancient World

The lines from "The Quadroon Girl," by Henry Wadsworth Longfellow, first appeared in *The Complete Works of Henry Wadsworth Longfellow* (Boston: Ticknor & Fields, 1866).

Information on the case of May Fielding comes from the article "May Fielding, the White Slave Girl," by Elizabeth Baker, published in *Epitaph* (Friends of Mount Hope Cemetery newsletter)31, no. 1 (Winter 2011).

Mary Jo Lanphear, Brighton Town historian, provided helpful information on Celestia Bloss via correspondence and "Notes from a Talk on Celestia Angenette Bloss," delivered at the Susan B. Anthony House, Rochester, New York, 2007.

Information on the Bloss Family comes from the *Encyclopedia of Biography of New York: A Life Record of Men and Women Whose Sterling Character and Energy and Industry Have Made Them Preëminent in Their Own and Many Other States*, vol. 4, by Charles Elliott Fitch (New York: American Historical Society, 1916).

The Opposite of Fear

The epigraph is taken from *East of Eden*, by John Steinbeck (New York: Viking Press, 1952).

Human Curiosity: A Circular Concordance

Information is taken from "Circus Folk Mourn 'Best-Liked Freak': Krao, the "Missing Link' Buried with Tribute of Tears from Side-Show Associates," *New York Times*, April 19, 1926, and "Krao, the Human Monkey," *New York Times*, February 8, 1883.

Information on William Hunt aka Farini comes from *The Great Farini*, by Shane Peacock (Toronto: Allen Lane/Penguin, 1995).

Lyrics from "Jerusalem the Golden," by Bernard of Cluny (twelfth century), and translated from Latin by John M. Neale, 1858. Available online at http://www.cyberhymnal.org/htm/j/t/jtgolden/htm.

The Second Morning

All italicized text is taken from the story "Beyond the Bayou," by Kate Chopin, in *Bayou Folk* (Boston: Houghton Mifflin, 1894).

Blue Kentucky Girl

Information about Luna and the Fugates comes from "The Blue People of Troublesome Creek: The Story of an Appalachian Malady, an Inquisitive Doctor, and a Paradoxical Cure," by Cathy Trost, *Science* 82 (November 1982). Available online at http://www.indiana.edu/~oso/lessons/Blues/TheBlues.htm.

The Other Magpie

The epigraph is taken from "Why I Am Pagan," by Zitkala-Ša (Gertrude Bonnin) from *Atlantic Monthly*, December 1902, 801–3.

Information on Zitkala-Ša's childhood comes from *American Indian Stories*, by Zitkala-Ša (Washington, D.C.: Hayworth Publishing House, 1921) and *Dreams and Thunder: Stories, Poems, and The Sun Dance Opera*, by Zitkala-Ša, edited by P. Jane Hafen (Lincoln: University of Nebraska Press, 2001).

Information on The Other Magpie at the Battle of the Rosebud comes from *Pretty-shield: Medicine Woman of the Crows*, by Frank D. Linderman (New York: Harper Collins, 1932; repr., Lincoln: University of Nebraska Press, 1974).

Return to the Dreamland

The epigraph is taken from "To a Young Poet," by Edna St. Vincent Millay, from *Collected Poems* (New York: Harper Collins, 1956).

The two lines of poetry come from "At Baia," by H.D., in *Hymen* (London: Egoist Press, 1921) and "Harlem," by Langston Hughes, in *The Collected Poems of Langston Hughes* (New York: Vintage Books, 1995).

Information on the old Dreamland Park, including the dance hall, is based on reports by Matthew Caulfield, local historian (Irondequoit, New York), shared in public presentations and online at http://www.Rochestersubway.com.